Whispers

Karen,

<My grandmother
taught me that God
doesn't shout to us
He Whispers to
that I've near Hii

Viie

Love, Kim

Whispers in The Silent Space

By Lyla Campbell

There is a space down in our soul
A Silent Space to be made whole.
Where life's painful memories have taken their toll.
We begin to ask, "What's that sound deep in our soul?"
Suddenly we realize life is passing by
And the silent space begins to cry.
Now the space starts to shout,
"Where are you Lord?" Our soul cries out.
When we feel like Job
And our life has been hit by a twister,
Then quietly you speak in a gentle soft whisper.
"My love for you will fill the space
With Joy and laughter of amazing grace."
When the whisper becomes faint and hard to cope,
Ask the Lord to restore your hope.
Hope in His whispers for wisdom and direction
To allow Him to correct you so you can live in His perfection.
Now once again, our space is still
In Total peace by surrendering our will.
Listening to Your whispers of love deep in our soul
What was a broken and silent space
Has been made whole.

A JOURNEY INTO HEARING GOD'S VOICE

by Kim Wear

Christian Literature & Artwork
A BOLD TRUTH Publication

BOLD TRUTH PUBLISHING
(Christian Literature & Artwork)
606 West 41st, Ste. 4
Sand Springs, Oklahoma 74063
www.BoldTruthPublishing.com
beirep@yahoo.com

Available from Amazon.com and other retail outlets. Orders by U.S. trade bookstores and wholesalers.

Quantity sales special discounts are available on quantity purchases by corporations, associations, and others. For details, contact the publisher at the address above.

Cover Art, Layout & Design by Aaron Jones

Printed in the USA.

11 17   10 9 8 7 6 5 4 3 2 1

Contents

Introduction

Do you find it Amazing that The God who created the heavens and the earth desires that we, His creation would become His children? And if we become God's children then that makes Him—our Father.

Something I find equally breathtaking and beautiful is the fact that He has written His children's names in the palm of His hand. *Isaiah 49:16.* Your name is not only written in the Lamb's Book of Life But also in The Palm of The Creator's Hand.

How special and wonderfully awesome is that? Evidence of His ability to be THE Magnificent ONE and Daddy too. How fierce is His Love For Us. Signifying that We are Loved and deeply cared for and safely protected in His Hand.

If this is true, would it be so hard to believe that He would speak to us? Not as some would only teach about sin or wrongdoing and I do believe that, but even that His correction is done with the deepest affection. That He not only speaks or as I call it, 'Whispers' to bring correction but to guide us in the affairs of life both in Earth and Heaven.

Would He talk to you about a good hairdresser? Would He lead You to the right home and mortgage broker? Would he answer your cry for help as it relates to a job or a trying child? My ANSWER is Yes, Yes, Yes. I have asked for these answers and received them.

Whispers is to help your heart Trust and develop Faith in God's willingness to whisper Love, Answers, Revelation, etc. to His Children's Hearts.

Oh Woman of God,

Imagine with me a time when you are able to sit back and relax. After all you do get those times, right? It was in a time just like it that I had the opportunity to hear for a moment a definitive whisper in my ear. It wasn't someone asking me a question or telling me a secret. In fact it was far greater. My head was spinning and my body was tired, but I needed a word that would speak into my life.

Every time when I am in this place, that is exactly what I get. It is how I do my life with God. Let me make it clear to you: it wasn't in my actual ear that I heard these Whispers, instead it was by His spirit in my spirit, that He spoke and I heard Him. Oh how I love to hear the Voice of my Heavenly Father.

In this devotional I have taken the time to get His direction into what I should say and how best to say it. I believe that in order for you to be successful in your everyday life it requires you to live standing by His side. God created you. He wants to do this Life with you. He loves you. He desires to whisper in your ear. My dear friend, Lyla Campbell, wrote a special poem for this book found in the front of this book. It speaks directly to your need of hearing the whispers of God in your life.

Each section contains insights in how to deal with what is facing you. Don't just read through this book and think you have it made. Instead, take each devotional as an assignment for your life. Purpose in your heart to hear what the Holy Spirit is speaking to you and then do it. Not just one time. Continue in it until it becomes a part of who you are as a mighty Woman of God. Each whisper includes a call to action and a space to journal what He has whispered to you.

Love,
Kim Wear

Section 1

Out with the Old, In with the New!

"Therefore, if anyone is in Christ, He is a new creation;
old things Have passed away, behold,
All things have become new."

— 2 Corinthians 5:17 NKJV

"There is no pit so deep,
that God's love is not deeper still."

— Corrie Ten Boom

Whisper One

It makes no difference what you think you have done, there is hope. It is not a false promise, but a real fact. Your mind replays continually the mistakes made and your heart condemns you. Trying to look good on the outside and make others believe you are okay is wearing you thin. What does God in His Word have to say about your condition?

1 John 3:20-23 says,

> *"For if our heart condemns us, God is greater than our heart, and knows all things. Beloved, if our heart doesn't condemn us, we have confidence toward God. And whatever we ask we receive from Him, because we keep His commandments and do those things that are pleasing in His sight. And this is His commandment: that we Should believe on the name of His Son Jesus Christ and love another, as He gave us commandment."*

I kept hearing the Holy Spirit whisper over and over again to tell you, *"That My Grace is Greater. My Love is Greater than your weakness, than your sin. My love is abundant. The blood of Christ flows toward you today. Rise up. Quit beating yourself up."* He says to you, *"Yes I know what you did and yes of course you should not have done that, but that is what forgiveness is for. That is what mercy is for."*

A Call to Action

Receive it, receive it right now. In fact lift your hands and begin to receive His love towards you. Say with your mouth, *"Lord I thank you for your love. I thank you that your blood cries out for mercy. That you* are faithful to forgive. I ask for forgiveness and I receive your love and forgiveness." Now receive His cleansing for your sin. *1 John 1:9* tells us that if we confess our sins He is faithful and just to forgive and cleanse us. Come to the fountain of life and let Him cleanse you from your mistakes. Say this: Lord cleanse me from my sin. Cleanse me from this self condemnation. Heal me and I will be healed. Receive it. Now forgive yourself, because the Great I am forgives you, then you have no business holding onto it. Don't allow Satan to speak to you again about what you have been forgiven of. Shut the door to that right now.. Hallelujah, His grace is sufficient and His love is abundant!

> *"The attacks on your life have much more to do with who you might be in the future than who you have been in the past."*
>
> — Lisa Bevere

Notes

_____

_____

_____

_____

_____

_____

_____

_____

_____

_____

Whisper Two

Earlier in my life when I first started out as an adult, the world was before me and nothing was going to stop me. I had hopes. I had plans. I had dreams. Then life began to happen. There were a few times that what I planned didn't seem to be going quite the way I had envisioned them. I kept moving forward. Then before I knew it my hopes, plans and dreams were crushed like a tin can. The attacks on my life became overwhelming. It seemed as if I couldn't fix what was going on in my life. Instead it was turning me inside out. Then I came to a complete stop.

Genesis 1:26-27 says,

> *"Then God said, 'Let us make man in Our Image, according to Our likeness; let them have dominion, over the fish of the sea, over the birds of the air, and over the cattle, over all the earth and over every creeping thing that creeps on the earth. So God created man in His own image; in the image of God He created him; male and female He created them."*

What do these Scriptures have to do with the attacks that are thwarting our dreams? Everything. You see God thought of you first and then He created you. He placed destiny in your hearts. He placed Adam in a garden, that was his destiny? He went on and gave us dominion in this life. But the best part is found in the end of the verses: *"...male and female He created them."* We were created like God. To look like Him, Have dominion in the earth, to rule and reign. Then in *Genesis 2*, Satan came and ruined EVERYTHING. God's plan for His man and woman, derailed. Don't take the attacks, the trips and drips on your life - personal. You are not a loser. Quite the opposite. You Are God's daughter.

Listen sister, God created you. He knows the plans and purposes for your life and He knows how to fix you and get your life back on track.

A Call to Action

In order to be restored from our broken pasts we first and foremost have to go back to the One Who created us. What do you do if your computer or smart phone is not working? Especially when you've done all you know to do? Maybe you tried taking it from place to place to get it fixed. Ultimately it required being sent back to the manufacturer for repair. Why? It's because they were the author of your device.

Today go to the Author of your life. God, Jesus and the Holy Spirit are expecting your arrival. They have hopes, plans and dreams just waiting to be rebooted and made alive again. Call upon them in prayer!

Notes

Whisper Three

The road in your life can be extremely hard at times, especially with all of the ups and downs or twists and turns. How often have you tried to navigate through them all by yourself? *Listen to me: you were never made to try to figure it out on your own.* You know the One Who has the way all figured out. He knows where to turn and how to get back up again—He will be with you through it all.

That brings me to my next point. In ups and downs or twists and turns your why's do one of two things, it either creates a fork in the road that God has set for you or it gives you an opportunity to embrace the character of God; your choice. When you trust Him, He reveals Who He is to you; get to know Him. Be convinced of these things and when the enemy tries to get you off the path that God has for you, you won't even consider the why's. Instead, you will be fully persuaded and convinced that HE IS GOOD.

Proverbs 3:5 says,

> "Trust God from the bottom of your heart; don't try to figure out everything on your own. Listen for God's voice in everything you do, everywhere you go; he's the one who will keep you on track."

A Call to Action

Have you embraced you? There is a reason you were born! Are you still looking for why you are you? Jesus knew what He was put here to do on this earth. He knew why He was born; He went on and fulfilled that purpose.

Don't you think it is time for you to know your purpose? Remember that the devil isn't the only one moving in your life. God is too and He already won the victory for you in His Son, Jesus Christ!   You just keep your focus on God in all things that pertain to this life. *James 5:7-8* teaches that Jesus is waiting for the precious fruit of the harvest in the same way that farmers do after their crops have been planted. His return isn't delayed—it is right on schedule. You are a part of that amazing harvest. God's plan for your life includes seeing you through every up and down or twist and turn! He loves you.

No matter what you have been through in life, God's plan isn't delayed. The trouble and sorrow in this world will never be greater than His promise of strength in you. Say it with your mouth: *"God's plan for me isn't delayed by ups and downs or twist and turns. I choose to trust in Him. I am fully persuaded and convinced that He is good. Just like Jesus I know my plan, my purpose and it will be said of me that I fulfilled it."*

Notes

_____

_____

_____

_____

_____

_____

_____

_____

_____

_____

_____

Whisper Four

I am reminded by the Lord often, to spend time in fellowship with Him. I do that by reading the precious Word of God daily. It doesn't stop there. As I mentioned in the opening of this devotional, I wait to hear what He whispers in my ear. The ear of my spirit. If I choose not to fellowship with Him in the Word of God and prayer then I assure you I would be a different person.

1 John 1:6-7 says,
> *"If we say that we have fellowship with Him, and walk in darkness, we lie, and do not the truth: But if we walk in the light, as he is in the light, we have fellowship one with another, and the blood of Jesus Christ his Son cleanseth us from all sin."*

I had a conversation with someone who formerly lived a life of addiction. This person proclaimed Jesus Christ as the Lord of their life. I said to this person, *"When did you come to the Lord?"* They responded immediately, *"I never left."* I tell you this story because this person was convinced that their life of darkness didn't affect their fellowship with Christ. If you walk in darkness you lie and do not practice the truth. I didn't say it, the Bible did.

The truth of the Word of God can't be altered or it is no longer *"The Truth!"* Jesus is the standard for all truth. Therefore, it is not what you or I think, that makes something a truth. He is the truth and we now walk in the light of all that truth; it defines who you are in Christ!

God desires fellowship, and you say that you want an intimate relationship with Him. But are you fellowshipping with darkness or light? There is a requirement for that sweet fellowship: it is walking in the light as He is in the light. There really is fellowship with truth and the blood of Jesus cleanses you and I from ALL SIN as we walk in the light of Christ. There is grace for whatever you need.

A Call to Action

Align your thoughts and actions to what the Word of God actually says. Not what you think it says. Spend time everyday on purpose with God in His Word and by speaking with Him through prayer. Don't just be the one doing all the talking. STOP, WAIT and Listen to what the precious Holy Spirit will whisper into the ear of your spirit—then do what He says!

> *"Our pursuit of God can be successful just because He is forever seeking to manifest Himself to us."*
> — A.W. Tozer

Notes

_____

_____

_____

_____

_____

_____

_____

_____

_____

_____

_____

Whisper Five

Are you able to recall the last time someone asked you what you were passionate about? How did you answer them? Did anyone ever tell you that your passive? How did you respond? Passionate or Passive! In reality the choice is yours. Let me ask you another question, *"Are you passionate or passive about your salvation?"* Before you answer think about what these words mean.

Passionate as defined by the Merriam-Webster dictionary says: having, showing, or expressing strong emotions or beliefs. It can also mean: fired with intense feeling; ardent, blazing, burning or obsolete suffering; sorrowful.

Passive as defined by the Merriam-Webster dictionary says: used to describe someone who allows things to happen or who accepts what other people do or decide without trying to change anything. It can also mean being subjected to an action without producing a reaction. I say it as one who takes no action.

Salvation as defined by Wiktionary says: the process of being saved, the state of having been saved (from Hell). The process of being restored or made new for the purpose of becoming saved; the process of being rid of the old poor quality conditions and becoming improved.

I will ask you again, *"Are you passionate or passive about your Salvation?"* I am passionate about my salvation experience. It is strong, blazing and burning within me. I discovered my precious Lord Jesus Christ and I have not looked back to my old ways again. He grabbed my attention and captured my heart. I am His and He is mine.

Philippians 3:12 says,

> *"Not that I have already attained, or am already perfected; but I press on, that I may lay hold of that for which Christ Jesus has also laid hold of me."*

A Call to Action

Commit yourself to express your strong belief in Christ. Strengthen your belief by spending time in the Word of God and in fellowship with God. Say this out loud with me, *"I am strong in my beliefs. I will be a blazing burning light to the darkness around me. My salvation experience has gotten rid of the old poor qualities I once had and now I am made new in Christ. My life is no longer subjected to inaction. I put the devil on notice that I am a mighty Woman of God."*

Notes

Whisper Six

1 Timothy 4:8 says,

"For bodily exercise profits a little, but godliness is profitable for all things, having promise of the life that now is and of that which is to come."

The previous Whispers started with forgiveness that lead to restoration. From there you learned to trust God and move into fellowship with Him. Then you determined your reaction to salvation and what it would look like.

Now here you are today and I want to challenge you with a quote from Charles Spurgeon.

He said, *"I assure you, and there are thousands of my brethren who can affirm the same. That after having tried the ways of sin, we infinitely prefer the ways of righteousness for their own pleasure's sake even here, and we would not change with ungodly men even if we had to die like dogs. With all the sorrow and care which Christian life is supposed to bring, we would prefer it to any other form of life beneath the stars."*

God intended for your life to be lived with Him. It is why I have written this devotional *"Whispers."* Timothy has great insight into our lives. When you serve God it is profitable for you and those around you, but it doesn't stop there—you are an eternal being!

The life of God on the inside of you is the same power that God used to raise Christ from the dead. The ways of sin can't even begin to compare to the ways of righteousness and the power that brings in your life. No matter your circumstances God has a promise for the life you are living.

A Call to Action

Speak this to yourself out loud and as you do commit to live your life beneath the stars unlike any other time in your life.

There is a remedy for every sin sick soul. There is a solution for all the problems deep inside. There is a remedy and His Name is Jesus Christ. I thank God for the blood of Jesus for it bought my salvation from sin. Healing for my body. A sound mind and sound emotions. Protection, power, authority and restoration. It is what God demanded for my salvation. Nothing else would get it for me but only the precious blood of Jesus!

Notes

Whisper Seven

Have you ever stood in a place prepared to be revealed? As one standing behind a curtain right before a play. All dressed up to go on a date or even right before an interview. You know it as well as I do, that much work went into the preparation for that reveal. Oh mighty Woman of God, if we can do that for the approval of man (our peers) how much more does God desire to reveal Himself to you?

One of the most important roles the Holy Spirit plays in your life is the revealer of truth. There are some truths that must have a greater intensity, a greater revelation than you just knowing it in your mind. I believe the greatest revelation you will ever need to know is Jesus being your Lord and Savior.

John 16:13 says,

> *"However, when He, the Spirit of truth, has come, He will guide you into all truth; for He will not speak on His own authority, but whatever He hears He will speak; and He will tell you things to come."*

The disciples walked with Jesus, they ate with Jesus, they worked alongside Jesus in the ministry, they even fished with Jesus. However, one day Jesus asked them, *"Who do men say that I am?"* After they answered, He asked to them, *"But who do you say that I am?"* It was Peter who said, *"You are the Christ."* (cf. Mark 8:27-30) If Peter, who knew Jesus in the flesh needed the great revelator to know Jesus as the Son of the Living God—then we need Him too.

A Call to Action

Revelation is much deeper than head knowledge gained from your personal studying. It is revealed truth that sets you free. It unlocks the truth in us. I believe that if we really knew Who we are serving and calling our Lord, we would be and live differently. Ask the precious Holy Spirit today to reveal the Lord Jesus to you.

I heard this down on the inside, a whisper: *"The curtain is about to part and Jesus Christ our Lord and Risen King is about to take center stage. The world is going to know the Lord we serve! He is going to reveal Himself to this lost, darkened sinful world. Glory to God!"*

Notes

_____

_____

_____

_____

_____

_____

_____

_____

_____

_____

_____

_____

Whisper Eight

"Worry does not empty tomorrow of its sorrow,
it empties today of its strength." - Corrie Ten Boom

In this life there is sorrow and disappointment. I remember when I was a younger woman, I hated adversity; I had so much of it. In fact I was afraid of it. I would start worrying about the situations right in front of me. I didn't realize that I was robbing my *"today"* of its needed strength and adding *"unnecessary sorrows for my tomorrows."*

2 Corinthians 4:16 says,

"Therefore we do not lose heart. Even though our outward man is perishing, yet the inward man is being renewed day by day."

I don't know about you, but I need strength today. It's a precious commodity that God gives new each day. When I allowed the revelation of 2 Corinthians 4:16 to enter into my life I discovered the peace that comes with *"The Plan",* not *"a"* plan—but *"His Plan."* I am no longer afraid of adversity. I have seen the Lord take what I have walked through and forge a strength in me, despite the pain, He forged wisdom in spite of sorrow.

I want you to get this down on the inside of you: *"He made me a weapon forged in the fires of adversity."* When I learned to trust Him and love Him through the trial, that is when He was able to make all things turn out for my good. I didn't say, *"He made a weapon."* I said, *"He made me a weapon."* There's a huge difference!

The death of my beloved husband Gregg Wear was reason enough for me to have worried and any permission I needed to have sorrowed. Yet on the inside of me, I heard a Whisper that: I chose to listen to and obey. The precious Holy Spirit said, *"Right now your life looks like a maze. You do not know your way out of this. But from my vantage point I can see you just fine. If you follow my voice and listen to my directives I will lead you out. If I say go left, then go left. If I say go the right, then go to the right. I will lead you out of this place and into a new place that I have already prepared for you."*

A Call to Action

The word *reach* implies extending or stretching. God has made all things from His Word accessible to you. It's within your reach and capabilities, but you have to reach for it. The Woman who brings the greatest effect and the most lasting contribution to Earth: is the Woman that walks with God. Listen to Him, and He will show you the way and give you strength that is renewed day by day. Be the mighty weapon that God designed you to be!

Notes

Whisper Nine

Revelations 12:10-11 says,

"Then I heard a loud voice saying in heaven, "Now salvation, and strength, and the kingdom of God, and the power of His Christ have come, for the accuser of our brethren, who accused them before our God day and night, has been cast down. And they overcame him by the blood of the Lamb and by the word of their testimony, and they did not love their lives to the death."

I am so thankful for the blood of Jesus. I am so thankful that the blood cries out on your behalf—Mercy! That same blood bought your salvation from sins and healing for your body. It provides a sound mind, sound emotions, protection, power, authority and restoration. Your victory comes from the blood, but it's enforced by your testimony. That means you have to speak.

Oh Woman of God, we have a mutual enemy who interrogates our every decision. The devil is a bully and he likes to pick fights. He wants to fight you. Not the God inside of you, just you. He knows that he doesn't stand a chance if God takes the ring. Put God in your ring today. Let Him fight for you.

A Call to Action

When Satan reminds you of your mistakes, You remind him of his future. Jesus said that the devil is a thief, murderer and a liar. When he interrogates you, those thoughts will fall into one or all three of the categories. Don't let him speak to you or he will rob you of your future. He will steal your healing. He will kill your joy. Think about what you are thinking because your thoughts will lead you.

Say this with me: Satan I don't serve you. You got served 2,000 years ago by the One I love and by the One I serve. Jesus Christ, my Lord. He loved me and released me from sin by His precious blood. He released you of your assignment against me and your rule in my life. I now sit with Him in Heavenly Places and have authority over you in all arenas of my life.

Today, I challenge you to share your testimony of Christ with someone who the precious Holy Spirit will reveal to you.

Notes

_____

_____

_____

_____

_____

_____

_____

_____

_____

_____

_____

_____

_____

Whisper Ten

Revelations 12:10-11 says,

"Then I heard a loud voice saying in heaven, "Now salvation, and strength, and the kingdom of God, and the power of His Christ have come, for the accuser of our brethren, who accused them before our God day and night, has been cast down. And they overcame him by the blood of the Lamb and by the word of their testimony, and they did not love their lives to the death."

I absolutely love this Scripture and I need to repeat it again today. At the end of your life this Scripture reveals the way God looks at your life here on Earth. He is not looking for perfection. He is not even looking for those that have never made any mistakes.

God is not shocked and He isn't disappointed because of a darkened season in your life, when in a moment of weakness you succumbed to Satan's strategies of deception. This Scripture clearly reveals that you are in the fight of your life. Remember I said, *"Our mutual enemy interrogates our every decision."* The only weapon he has to use against you is your past. Oh, it is why I love the blood of Jesus. It disarms the devil of his only tool.

I just heard this down on the inside, a whisper for you from the precious Holy Spirit:

"Now salvation has come! I have YOU, all safe and sound with me, your Father. I look at all of my children and I clap! Well done. YOU made it despite that divorce, or death of your child or husband. YOU overcame the hater of your soul. That enemy who works relentlessly to get you to just give up. He lied to you and deceived you, but YOU kept coming back to Me. YOU kept getting up and tighten-

ing the belt of truth. YOU secured your shoes of evangelism. YOU continued to bring the Good News. YOU put up YOUR shield of faith. Through the tears and the bleeding wounds YOU kept swinging your sword, which is the Word of God. YOU enforced My Word. YOU kept speaking your testimony. By standing your ground, YOU enforced the victory of My Son. YOU stayed engaged in the fight of faith. Now you are with ME."

A Call to Action

I have come to the conclusion that man cannot be pleased, BUT GOD can. There is a saying that, *"God forgives sins that man won't."* Take a new look at yourself today in light of *Revelations 12:10-11.* As you do, you are going to see a different person. See yourself as the one who overcame by the blood of the Lamb and whose testimony is now that of one whose Lord is Jesus Christ.

"Don't worry about the people in your past; there is a reason they didn't make into your future."
- Adam Lindsay Gordon

Notes

_____

_____

_____

_____

_____

_____

_____

Whisper Eleven

I was thinking about the way Jesus came into the world, born in a manger and not in a Marriott. The way He came was a representation of His character and life. He was humble and meek. He stripped Himself of all His nobility, power and might. He gave up being with Almighty God. He was utterly obedient, even to the extent of dying.

Hebrews 12:2 NASB says,
> *"fixing our eyes on Jesus, the author and perfecter of faith, who for the joy set before Him endured the cross, despising the shame, and has sat down at the right hand of the throne of God."*

He stooped so low to pick us up to where He was and is again. He was God and man. He did that to touch and save all of humanity. Can you and I not also humble ourselves to do the same thing? Ask the precious Holy Spirit to make you as humble in Jesus Christ? Walk as He walked to reach this fallen man, so that the Lamb Who was slain will receive His just reward.

A Call to Action

Think about what Jesus did for you. Think about what He did for all mankind. Fix your eyes and your thoughts on the Lord and Saviour. Be mindful of His Redemptive work today. This statement will come in handy to assist you in your rejoicing:

> *Let the just rejoice,*
> *For their justifier is born.*
> *Let the sick and infirm rejoice,*

For their saviour is born.
Let the captives rejoice,
For their Redeemer is born.
Let slaves rejoice,
For their Master is born.
Let free men rejoice,
For Jesus Christ is born.
- St. Augustine of Hippo (AD 354-440)

Jesus sat down at the right hand of the throne of God because He completed His work. E.W. Kenyon says, *"The fact is a receipt."* Glory to God say this with me: *"I am free. I am healed. He broke the dominion of the enemy forever. That is the conclusion of the whole matter!"* Get busy fulfilling the work Christ has placed in you to do.

Notes

_____

_____

_____

_____

_____

_____

_____

_____

_____

_____

_____

Section 2

Mirror, Mirror Who is.......?

*"But be doers of the word, and not hearers only, deceiving yourselves.
For if anyone is a hearer of the word and not a doer,
he is like a man observing his natural face in a mirror;
for he observes himself, goes away, and immediately forgets what
kind of man he was. But he who looks into the perfect law of liberty
and continues in it, and is not a forgetful hearer but a doer of the
work, this one will be blessed in what he does."*

— James 1:22-25

*"Our pursuit of God can be successful just because He is
forever seeking to manifest Himself to us."* – A. W. Tozer

Whisper Twelve

Joshua 1:8 says,

"This Book of the Law shall not depart from your mouth, but you shall read [and meditate on] it day and night, so that you may be careful to do [everything] in accordance with all that is written in it; for then you will make your way prosperous, and then you will be successful. (Amplified)

The Word is the power of God. It brings forth power to the situation that you need help with. You will gain wisdom to know how to deal wisely with people in any situation. When you speak His Word, it's like a sword cutting away and slaying the works of the devil. God desires for you to be successful. Your success is found in the Word.

Yet there are some who do not hearken to the Word of truth. It is evident by how their lives are lived. Oh Woman of God, don't be like those who do not hearken to the Word. Instead, be like those who determined to live a life of faith in God.

The word *canon* comes to mind as I think about *Joshua 1:8*. The Strong's Concordance defines this word in the Greek language as, *"a rod (bar) used as a measuring standard, originally, a cane or reed."* Imagine a reed that grows straight enough that it can be used as a measuring stick. A *canon* is the standard norm. In that same manner, *Truth* is the standard norm of God. He has a *standard of truth* that must not be diluted or lowered. You would do well to come up and walk with Him in truth.

God desires to speak to you about many things. Your mind-set, thoughts, beliefs, weaknesses, instability, wrong passions and wrong visions to name a few. Often times these are things that have held you back and prevented you from moving in time with the Holy Spirit. Do you understand how amazing it would be to be in time with God's perfect will for your life?

A Call to Action

The fulfillment you desire in life comes from a real relationship with Christ and your commitment to be in the Word. That is where the deepest peace and greatest joy can be found. Your discovery of God becomes the canon in your life. Remember this: The Word of God is always the same. What you are surrounded with right now can and will change, but God's Word never changes.

Take the Word of God just as Joshua did, speak it continually, meditate on it often. Be careful to DO what you have heard—then and only then will you make your way prosperous and successful.

Notes

_____

_____

_____

_____

_____

_____

_____

_____

_____

_____

Whisper Thirteen

This is for someone (it really is for all who will believe). These are not words just written on a page. They are Words of Life to any situation you are going through.

Psalms 91:1-16 says,

[He who dwells in the secret place of the Most High shall abide under the shadow of the Almighty. I will say of the Lord, "He is my refuge and my fortress; my God, in Him I will trust." Surely He shall deliver you from the snare of the fowler and from the perilous pestilence. He shall cover you with His feathers, and under His wings you shall take refuge; His truth shall be your shield and buckler. You shall not be afraid of the terror by night, nor of the arrow that flies by day, nor of the pestilence that walks in darkness, nor of the destruction that lays waste at noonday. A thousand may fall at your side, and ten thousand at your right hand; but it shall not come near you. Only with your eyes shall you look, and see the reward of the wicked. Because you have made the Lord, who is my refuge, even the Most High, your dwelling place, no evil shall befall you, nor shall any plague come near your dwelling; for He shall give His angels charge over you, to keep you in all your ways. In their hands they shall bear you up, lest you dash your foot against a stone. You shall tread upon the lion and the cobra, the young lion and the serpent you shall trample underfoot. Because he has set his love upon Me, therefore I will deliver him; I will set him on high, because he has known My name. He shall call upon Me, and I will answer him; I will be with him in trouble; I will deliver him and honor him. With long life I will satisfy him, and show him My salvation."]

A Call to Action

In those few passages there are over 20 promises that God guarantees He will do for you if you dwell in Him. There are benefits in store for you as you abide in Him. The key is that they are in Him.

If you are looking for a solution to what you are dealing with right now, it won't be found outside of the Word or outside of God. The distractions of this life can cause you to move out of your place in Him. You must discipline yourself to immediately go to Him first with everything. Listen for the whisper He wants to share with you.

Today, commit yourself to be a woman of God who accepts these 20 promises. Be the one who finds herself in the presence of Almighty God. I encourage you to spend some time right now by hiding *Psalms 91* in your heart. How do you do that? By speaking this Word over and over again until it becomes a reality on the inside of you.

Notes

Whisper Fourteen

When I teach on *Psalms 91* in meetings I place an emphasis on, *"he who dwells in the secret place."* What is this secret place? In the movie based off of Frances Hodgson Burnett's book *"The Secret Garden."* I recall the garden that Mary discovers on a large estate that she was forced to move to. It was in that garden that the characters Colin, Dickon and Mary found great peace and healing.

Unlike the fictional story, there is a real secret place in our Father. That secret place is the very presence of God. The Throne Room of Your Father in Heaven. A place where Satan cannot touch you. A place where you can find the security you seek. It is your place of protection. Your place of healing. It is where you meet with the King of the Universe. A place to meet Jesus. How do you think this would change you?

When I was a little girl I would often get lost in our little grocery store where my Mom shopped. She would say to my little sister Jennifer and I, *"You both stay right here with me. You are not getting toys. We are here to get groceries."* Then it would happen, little Kimberly, that's me, would see something sparkly and it would divert my attention. Before I knew it I was away from my Mom. I would run up and down the aisles looking for her and my sister.

Not long ago the precious Holy Spirit gave me a great analogy. He reminded me of the childhood memory I mentioned above about being lost in the grocery store. He said to me, *"If you had been kidnapped, your mother would have cried and would have said, but she was right here with me."* He went on to tell me that yes I was in the store with my Mom, but I was not in her presence. If I had been I would not have been lost or even kidnapped if that were the case.

That is how it is with your special relationship in the Lord. You are to be found in Christ. In that special place. You might be in the Church. You might be in the Word. You might even call yourself a Christian. But if you do not live in His presence you are like I was as the lost girl: in the store but not with her mom.

A Call to Action

When a child is in the presence of their parents it would be very difficult for anyone to take that child away. When you are dwelling in the presence of God, the enemy does not have access to you. Pay special attention to *Psalms 91:1*, *"He who dwells"* not one who frequently visits, but *"He who dwells."* You are expected to dwell and abide in Him.

Notes

Whisper Fifteen

I trust your are sensing the importance of the priority the Word of God should have in your life. Along with His Word, His Presence will bring them alive to you. I have always been interested in the dynamics of how the Bible was written. In my research I found that the very first translation of the English Bible was initiated by John Wycliffe and then completed by John Purvey in 1388.

The Bible was written by 40 different authors over a period of 2000 years dating from 1500 BC to about 100 AD. The men wrote the Scriptures did so as they were given inspiration by God. Around 50 Bibles are sold every minute. It is the world's best selling book. There have been some 1 Billion Bibles sold at the time of this writing. That is not surprising since God inspired the Book Himself.

2 Timothy 3:16-17 says,

> *"All scripture is given by the inspiration of God, and is profitable for doctrine, for reproof, for correction, for instruction in righteousness, that the man of God may be complete, thoroughly equipped for every good work."*

God put a great amount of detail into the writing of His Word. The Word of God must become to you—literally the WORDS OF GOD. It was never meant to just be admired, it was meant to be believed; it will take the revealer of truth, the precious Holy Spirit, to help you with this. When you allow Him to help you, the Words found in the Bible begin to come alive to you and produce life in your situations.

A Call to Action

Begin to think of all the detail you put into your day. You and I could make a list that would go on forever. If we care about our day that much, how much more does our Father care about the detail of His Word in your life. These precious Words found in your Bible were arranged just for you. He cares about your yesterday, today and tomorrow. He cares about what you have been through, where you are now and what you will go through in the future. Before your life began, He put together His Word for you.

One day the Holy Spirit spoke these Words in my spirit (a whisper). He said, *"I am the Holy Spirit. I am wisdom. I wrote the Word so I know what it meant when I said everything, but most never ask My opinion about ANYTHING! I am your Teacher ask Me questions and I will answer you."*

This is the best advice ever. Put Him to work. Ask Him His opinion. Be quiet enough to listen and then do what He says for you to do.

Notes

Whisper Sixteen

The Word of God is the avenue that brings the power of God. It is important for you to understand that His power is not made manifest through wishing, begging or praying in fear. Yet these three ingredients, seem to be our go to option for getting the power of God moving in the midst of circumstances.

For the Thanksgiving and Christmas seasons I am often home and not out traveling to minister. It allows me time do what I do for the ones I love. I don't get the desired results I expect without the proper ingredients and preparations. It is the same with the Word and Power of God operating in your life.

His Word promises you His Power, His Peace and His Wisdom. To that you must add: faith, confession and time to study His Word for yourself. These three ingredients added to His power, peace and wisdom will bring forth the results God has promised and the results you desire.

1 John 5:14-15 says,
> *"and how bold and free we then become in His presence, freely asking according to His will, sure that He's listening. And if we're confident that He's listening, we know that what we've asked for is as good as ours."*

A Call to Action

No amount of prayer full of wishing, begging or fear has ever accomplished its intention. Prayer is good, but it must be prayed in faith.

Knowing that He is listening to you when you pray His Word. The Word of God just told us above, that He hears your prayers.

Hearing is the same as having. The only prayer He hears is the one prayed in faith and it only comes out of the written Word of God. It is important for you to place an emphasis on believing THE WORD.

There are many who *"enjoy"* reading the Bible. They may even *"admire"* it, but if they aren't mixing what they enjoy and admire with faith, then it is unreasonable to expect any results. The main ingredient that will cause faith to rise in you is belief. Believing that it is God's desire and willingness to demonstrate His power in your life.

That, Oh mighty woman of God will generate multiple whispers in your personal life. Take time today and change your recipe of doing things the way you're used to doing them and start by adding His ingredients into the circumstances of your life.

Notes

_____

_____

_____

_____

_____

_____

_____

_____

_____

Whisper Seventeen

E.W. Kenyon said, *"The mind is renewed by studying the Word and by acting upon it. One may study the Word for years, but if he does not act on it, live it, is not a doer of it, the mind is not renewed."* He really had a revelation of who he was and what he had in Christ. You would do a great service in your life by endeavoring to activate his advice.

Romans 12:2 says,

> *"And do not be conformed to this world, but be transformed by the renewing of your mind, that you may prove what is that good and acceptable and perfect will of God."*

I have said this many times: whoever has your thought life has YOU! God wants your mind and so does Satan. Whoever you lend your thinking to, you will mirror that in your life. Either the Kingdom of God: which is life, peace and joy or the kingdom of darkness which produces death, selfishness, lack of peace and much sorrow.

When you choose to renew your mind, *Romans 12:2* assures that it will transform your life. You will begin to see things the way God sees them. This will cause your thoughts to align with His and change your actions which will lead to the course of your life becoming more like Him. Soon you will come out of the darkness and into the light and have a new life which will produce a new you. This transformation will renew and make a happier more productive YOU!

A Call to Action

It is time for you to know who you are and what you have in Christ. You need to act upon what is revealed to you. Pay attention to the whispers in your heart as they line up to the Word of God; prove out what is good and acceptable. If you are going around the same mountain for the 10th time, then you're probably not paying enough attention to the whispers of the Holy Spirit. It is time for you to renew your mind to the Word of God and do it.

Oh woman of God this is a time to work with the Holy Spirit. He is going to start confronting weakness in you that keeps you going around the same mountain. He wants to make you strong; He wants to make you immovable so that you can stand against the devil and help bring in the greatest harvest of souls the Church will ever reap for Jesus our King.

Commit this day to be a woman who dedicates herself to time spent renewing the mind to His precious Word.

Notes

Whisper Eighteen

There was a day I heard this whisper from the Holy Spirit down on the inside of me. He said, *"Have a God Blessed, God Ordered, God Ordained Day, Today!"* Throughout this entire devotion it is my goal to help you become acquainted with God personally, Jesus intimately and to experience the working of the Holy Spirit in your devotional life. After all it is the kind of life that God designed for each one to live.

The word *"God"* *means, *"The sole Supreme Being, eternal, spiritual, transcendent, who is the Creator and ruler of all and is infinite in all attributes."* He is the object of our worship.

The word *"Blessed"* *means, *"Consecrated, sacred, holy, sanctified, worthy of adoration, reverence, worship, supremely favored, fortunate, blissfully happy, contented, bringing happiness and thankfulness."*

The word *"Ordered"* *means, *"A state in which all components or elements are arranged logically, comprehensibly, naturally, in succession, established, and a peaceful or harmonious condition."*

The word *"Ordained"* as defined by dictionary.com says, *"To invest, confer upon, enact, establish, decree, give orders, destine, order, command, select and appoint."*

Psalms 90:2 NLT says,
   "Before the mountains were born, before you gave birth to the earth and the world, from the beginning to the end, you are God."

* www.dictionary.com

A Call to Action

There isn't a day that God hasn't thought about YOU. He knows all about YOU and still wants to know YOU more. Let me ask YOU, is there a day YOU haven't thought about HIM? Do you know all there is about HIM? Do YOU want to know more of HIM?

No matter how hard you try to have a blessed, ordered or ordained day as described above, it will not be possible unless GOD is front of each step. You have tried with some success. You've had pieces of each definition, but I like what the Holy Spirit said when He whispered this to me. Each word had GOD before it.

Don't go another day without God!

Say this out loud: *"I will have a God Blessed, God Ordered, God Ordained Day, Today!"*

Notes

_____

_____

_____

_____

_____

_____

_____

_____

_____

Whisper Nineteen

It doesn't take very long for God to bring about a miracle or to place you in a new season of your life. In *2 Kings 7:1-20* we read how Israel's need was met overnight. Israel was in a famine, yes I said it, *"A FAMINE"* not a recession. It took one WORD from God and everything changed for them.

The prophet Elisha, a mighty Man of God, said under the unction of the Holy Spirit,

> *"Hear ye the word of the Lord; Thus saith the Lord, tomorrow about this time shall a measure of fine flour be sold for a shekel, and two measures of barley for a shekel, in the gate of Samaria."*
>
> *- 2 Kings 7:1*

When I read that verse the words *tomorrow about this time* bore witness to me on the inside. It became alive in my spirit. It was another Whisper that I heard from the Holy Spirit. It is impossible for a famine to end that quick, but with GOD ALL THINGS ARE POSSIBLE. What you speak out of your mouth contains power. When it is the Word of God then your situation will change.

2 Thessalonians 2:13 says,
> *"For this cause also we thank God without ceasing, because, when you received the word of God which you heard of us, you received it not as the word of men, but as it is in truth, the word of God, which effectually works also in you that believe."*

The Word works it's power in those that believe. The Word of God is the power of God; it carries all of His attributes. As you believe that Word, it begins to work for you so you don't have too! The Word of God is working for you. As you release it in faith it is going to raise valleys and lower mountains. Find Scriptures that speak to your situation and begin to—speak them over your life.

A Call to Action

With every fiber of my being I know that you are in a new season. Your change is here. Things are moving and you shall see it. Say this out loud with me, *"Tomorrow About This Time, according to (the Scripture that speaks to your circumstance) it shall be done and I know it shall be done because the Word of God is working mightily on my behalf."*

Notes

_____

_____

_____

_____

_____

_____

_____

_____

_____

_____

_____

_____

_____

Whisper Twenty

You just discovered that the words you speak, if aligned with the Word of God and mixed with belief, will change any circumstance you are facing. Words are extremely powerful and you have been given the keys of the Kingdom of Heaven: The Holy Bible!

Matthew 16:19 says,

> *"And I will give unto thee the keys of the kingdom of heaven: and whatsoever thou shalt bind on earth shall be bound in heaven: and whatsoever thou shalt loose on earth shall be loosed in heaven."*

Two words stand out in this verse: *bind* and *loose*. Do you tend to be an expert in being bound by what has been spoken over you and fail to release them through the power of the spoken Word? As a result of this, strongholds develop in your life.

A stronghold can be a thought or a belief and philosophy that you see as truth. In actuality, they are lies the enemy uses to keep you in bondage to sin and wrong thinking. At some point in time you and I have had wrong thoughts that have plagued our minds. Thoughts like: I am fat, I am ugly, I am stupid or I will never have anything. They have continued to play in your head like a broken record.

As a believer in Jesus Christ, I have found that the tie that binds you to these strongholds is *the power of agreement* with them. When you decide to no longer side with the lies of the enemy and bind up these words, it is in that moment that you enforce your victory over the forces of darkness. It is your responsibility to side with the Word of God.

When you do, it will restore you on the inside and you will live FREE. You will be FREE.

A Call to Action

There is not one person who has not been affected by the power of words. Isn't it time for you to bind up the wrong words that have been spoken in and over your life? Isn't it time for you to release them (loose)? You haven't the power in yourself to stop them from affecting your thoughts, but GOD does and He did. Our precious Lord and Saviour Jesus Christ paid for your freedom with His own precious blood. He defeated the enemy for you, so that you would have freedom over them. Then He gave you the written Word to study and read.

I am reminded of the lyrics of a song from the Heritage Singers that says, *"God said it, I believe it and that settles it for me."* Today I challenge you, to be in the power of agreement with God's Word. Take what He says, get it down on the inside of you until you believe it and then let the peace of God settle upon your circumstances. Speak His Words today!

Notes

Whisper Twenty-One

Did you know that God doesn't have good or bad days? He is the same everyday. He is committed to His Word. What He says, He will do. Selah (pause and think about that). I have found great confidence in just knowing that God will do what He said He will do. It has come about by seeing Him perform in my life what He whispered in my spirit.

I like what E.W. Kenyon said, *"Remember, your word is you!"* I expect God to be a doer of His own Word. Now what about you? Have you ever told someone that you would DO something for them and then not do it? Did your word change because it was a good day or a bad day? Regardless of your day, you must learn to say, *"I gave my word therefore I must keep it, no matter what it costs me."*

If your word is of no value to you, then you might begin to reason that the Word of God is of no value to you. You do not value your word when you say you will do something and do not follow through with it. You live in an environment where political leaders and others lie to you, so you learn to not value their words. Due to living this way, you and I have learned to not value God's Word.

The Bible is a Book of words. The Lord whispered to me once, that all He can offer to you or me is Words. He said, *"It is up to us to put value, faith and trust into His Words and that they contain HIS POWER."* Additionally He said, *"When you start valuing your own personal words by making them good, then you will start putting greater value on mine and as a result you will begin to see it work for you!"*

A Call to Action

Each one of us has been given a measure of faith. Your faith, however, can be hindered and rendered void if you hurt your conscience. *1 John 3:20-21* says, *"For if our heart condemn us, God is greater than our heart, and knoweth all things. Beloved, if our heart condemn us not, then have we confidence toward God."* It is a great thing to have boldness and confidence before God with a clear conscience. In the same manner it is a great thing to know that your words matter.

Today, Oh Woman of God, as you expect God to be a doer of His Word, then might you consider being one of yours. He always is the same. I just want to be more like Him and I challenge you to do the same by keeping your word. I believe that the devil is at our mercy when we *"truly"* believe God's Word. Put your value, faith and trust in His today.

Notes

Whisper Twenty-Two

Do you now understand the value of your words and the importance of God's Words to you? I then challenge you to preach the WORDS of Christ. Preach the same Gospel that Jesus preached.

Mark 16:20 says,

"*And they went forth, and preached every where, the Lord working with them, and confirming the word with signs following.*"

Maybe this is the reason for the lack of the power of God in your own life and in many churches today. Rev. Dinsdale T. Young said in October 1921, "*Brother preachers, preach the crucified Christ, morning, noon, and night. You may preach all else, but if you do not preach that, you are not preaching Good News; and it is Good News that the unhappy world wants.*"

Oh I hear you saying it right now, "*But I am not a preacher!*" Well let me tell you this, your life preaches something each day—it is the pulpit you stand behind everyday. So you might as well preach Christ morning, noon, and night. Oh Mighty Woman of our Lord Jesus Christ, we are living in the most exciting days of the Church. Light and Darkness are clashing in the realm of the spirit, and we are seeing it on a small scale in the natural.

I say by the Spirit of Grace: for if you could see this fight on the true level that it is on in the spirit, you would be more sober concerning the time and the day that you are living in. There is much at stake and I solemnly charge you in the presence of God and of Christ Jesus, Who is to judge the living and the dead, and by HIS appearing, and His Kingdom: PREACH THE WORD!!! *(cf. 2 Timothy 4:1-2)*

A Call to Action

Think about the words you speak each day.   Every time your mouth opens, you have the choice of letting the words be of God or your own.

I was reading an article about the most important forces in the universe by a scientist. When I completed the article, I heard the precious Holy Spirit say to me, *"The Most Powerful Force In The Universe is The Words Spoken in the Mouth of the Believer!"*

Let your words be those that come from the Word of God as you preach from the pulpit of your life to another person.   Preach the Word, as Timothy instructed you and I to do.

Notes

Whispers

Section 3

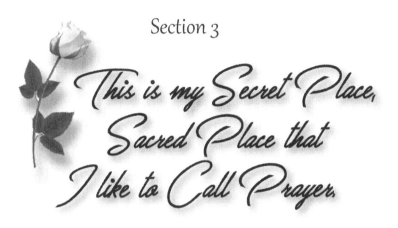

This is my Secret Place,
Sacred Place that
I like to Call Prayer.

"A prayer less Christian is a powerless Christian"
— Billy Graham

Whisper Twenty-Three

The more I know Him, the more I need Him. The more I need Him, the more I find myself loving Him. Oh Mighty Woman of God, you need Him more now than you ever have. I can't imagine, and I will not try to think of my life without Him. Can you say that about your relationship with the Lord Jesus Christ? What about your dependency upon the precious Holy Spirit? My, My, My, He is just so real to me.

If ever there was a time that we need to spend time praying, it is the days we live in right now. I will not live this life without spending my day in His presence. It is from that very secret, sacred place that I like to call prayer that every answer I have received comes from. It is where I go to get direction for my own personal life, for the ministry, and the words to speak to you in this devotional.

In this section, together, we will discover God's plan for praying for your personal life, your family (both in the natural and spiritual), your friends and equally as important your church and nation. I have a love for music and many times the Lord brings to my remembrance a revealed truth through them. At times, these become the very prayer I pray. There are other times that He reveals a truth that I then further study out to gain what it is He is speaking to me. You will see that throughout this devotional, but especially in this section of prayer.

How He speaks to me, is not necessarily how He will speak things to you. The key point is that you are developing a powerful prayer life with Him. Finding a special place that allows you the opportunity to hear what He is saying is crucial to your success as the Mighty Woman of God that you are.

A Call to Action

Designate an actual place today that becomes your consistent meeting spot with the Lord each day. Maybe it is special chair in your home. It might just be at the table with a hot cup of tea or coffee, but it is your place to meet with Him.

Matthew 22:37 says,
> "Jesus said unto him, Thou shalt love the Lord they God with all thy heart, and with all thy soul, and with all thy might."

From that place, become the powerful Christian that you need, your family needs, your friends, church and nation need. He is waiting for you right now.

Notes

Whisper Twenty-Four

One morning in my secret, sacred place the Lord Whispered in my spirit some words from a powerful Keith Green song. I had been seeking the Lord regarding the death of my beloved husband, Gregg. The Lord said to me, *"The less you need to know on this side, the more rewards await you on the other side."* The words of that song gave me great comfort.

Make My Life A Prayer - Keith Green

Make my life a prayer to you
I wanna do what you want me to.
No empty words and no white lies
No token prayers, no compromise.

I wanna share the light you gave
Through your Son you sent to save us
From ourselves and our despair
It comforts me to know that you're really there.

The Lord has a solution for everything that *"You"* are going through and He really wants you to get through to the other side. It's having to know every detail that sometimes will get in your way. It is then you must consecrate your will and life once again to God.

Proverbs 16:9 says,
"A man's heart deviseth his ways: but the Lord directeth his steps."

A Call to Action

You are not to go through this life with its twist and turns on a dark path with no light. You have a Father, Who wants to direct your steps and lead you in every phase of your life, ministry and business. You might ask where should I go? What shall I do? What is the right investment? What should I do about my child? What about my marriage? Where do I take the car to get it fixed?

I tell you that in all the years of my life on the face of this earth, I have asked our Father all of these questions. He has never failed to show me, when I prayed and took the steps on the right path that led me to my answer each time.

Take time right now and ask Him to show you the way regarding the questions you have for Him.

Notes

Whisper Twenty-Five

  It was in a time of prayer that I heard another Whisper from the Lord regarding the depths of my salvation. The words from the hymn *"Satisfied"* rose up in me and this is what it had to say:

"Satisfied" by Clara Tear Williams

Well of water, every springing,
Bread of Life, so rich and free,
Untold wealth that never faileth,
My redeemer is to me.

<u>Chorus:</u>
Hallelujah! I have found Him
Whom my soul so long has craved!
Jesus satisfies my longings;
Through His life I now am saved.

Shortly after this hymn rose up in me, the precious Holy Spirit reminded me of the Words He inspired that are found in the Book of Isaiah.

Isaiah 12:3 NIV says,
  "With joy you will draw water from the wells of salvation."

Isaiah 12:3 NLT says:
  "With joy you will drink deeply from the fountain of salvation."

He went on to say to me that *"Your tongue is the dipper."* How do you draw from a well? You must have a dipper. One of the most important ways you draw spiritually from the well of the spirit is with praise. It is a major part of my secret, sacred place I call prayer. As you praise Him, you will draw with joy, from Him. The joy comes many times after your praise. The more you do it the more joy you will bring up. The more life you will bring up. Spend time praising Him.

A Call to Action

Psalms 46:4 says,

"There is a river whose streams make glad the city of God, the holy place where the Most High dwells."

The Word of God says those streams are inside of "YOU!" It is the mighty Holy Spirit. Out of your belly SHALL FLOW R-I-V-E-R-S of living water. Heaven is in it all the time. You can too if you will just flow with HIM. Maybe you're in a season of drought. You're tired, thirsty and flat out broke. Trust me when I tell you, that if you would but spend time right now praising the One Who made you: you will find some deep waters from within you that will refresh everything and everyone around you.

Notes

Whisper Twenty-Six

The Lord speaks to me through music and as I was praying about this Whisper, the words from the hymn *"Draw Me Nearer"* came to me from Him and they are just for you.

"Draw Me Nearer" Fanny Crosby

I am thine, O Lord, I have heard Thy Voice,
And it told They Love to me;
But I long to rise in the arms of faith
And be closer drawn to Thee.

O the pure delight of a single hour
That before Thy throne I spend,
When I kneel in prayer, and with Thee, my God,
I commune as friend with friend!

In my prayer I asked God to grace us to come nearer and nearer to Him in prayer and fellowship and for you to rise up in faith. You are living in the end of the last days. Satan, your adversary, opposes you in your walk with God. He uses many tactics. The Bible clearly warns you to not be ignorant of the devil's devices. You are to be sober and alert. Ready at any moment.

Isaiah 61:3 instructs you to *"Put on the garment of Praise"* for the spirit of heaviness. This spirit of heaviness is sent to sift you of your hope, your power, and your will. Instead of accepting any of it, why don't you just PRAISE GOD! As you do that, the feelings and thoughts will evaporate. Or you could just do nothing and be overcome by the devices and tactics of the enemy for awhile. Don't be that foolish! Get your Praise on Today!

A Call to Action

Jude 1:20 NIV says,

> "But you, dear friends, build yourselves up in your most holy faith and pray in the Holy Spirit."

Ford has a motto: *"Built to Last."* That is how God made you, oh Mighty Woman of God. However, a believer will only be as strong as their prayer life. You must stay vitally connected to the vine of life: Jesus! Remain connected to Him throughout the day. Think of Him often. Love on Him. Depend upon Him. That is where you will find yourself missing it often. I challenge you to draw hard from His grace, His favor, and His ability to remain STRONG. You can not do it without Him. I challenge you to pray daily in the Holy Ghost! Praying like that in your secret sacred place; called (Prayer) is like revving up the engine in a race car. That kind of praying will keep you–strong, strong, strong. It will cause you to outlast the devil or any temptation.

Notes

Whisper Twenty-Seven

When people ask me how to pray, I respond by asking if they know how to talk to their best friend. Do you have that friend who you can tell anything to and know it will be safe in their heart? They're strong enough to hear your weaknesses, faults, failures and not fall apart! That is exactly what it is like when you or I pray to our Father in Heaven.

1 John 5:14-15 NKJV says,

> *"Now this is the confidence that we have in Him, that if we ask anything according to His will, He hears us. And if we know that He hears us, whatever we ask, we know that we have the petitions that we have asked of Him."*

Prayer is simply talking with God, like you would with your best friend. There are many different types of prayer, but they are still talking with Him. I am frequently asked by others, *"When do I pray?"* There is no right or wrong time to pray as in regards to the time of day or how many days to pray. The Holy Spirit, as He leads more and more of your life, will whisper those times in your heart.

According to the Scriptures above, there are two stipulations for your prayer to be heard and answered. When Jesus stood before the tomb of Lazarus, his prayer to the Father reinforced that God ALWAYS heard his prayers. Oh Woman of God, I know that I am talking to you, one who loves the Lord. I know am speaking to a woman who BELIEVES that God loves her and is able to do anything. Our mutual Father is mighty, but do you believe that He ALWAYS HEARS YOU WHEN YOU PRAY?

The second stipulations for answered prayers is for you to believe that

He heard you when you prayed. Hearing isn't necessarily a physical thing. God hears prayers and many other things. In the Bible, hearing means having or answering. The knowledge applied to your personal times of prayer will bring it to life. Just to know that He has and is answering your prayer is powerful.

A Call to Action

Say this with me: *"Father, I believe you're listening to me when I pray and that you are granting my requests, as long as they continue to line up with your Word."* I want you to think about the words from this song by Jim Reeves. For I believe they will bring comfort to you.

*"How long has it been? How long has it been
since you talked with the Lord
And told Him your heart's hidden secrets? How long since you prayed?
How long has it been since you stayed on your knees
till the light shone through?
How long has it been since your mind felt at ease?
How long since your heart knew no burden?
Can you call Him your friend? How long has it been
since you knew that He cared for you?"*

Notes

Whisper Twenty-Eight

James 1:5-7 NKJV says,

"If any of you lacks wisdom, let him ask of God, who gives liberally and without reproach, and it will be given to him. BUT LET HIM ASK IN FAITH, WITHOUT DOUBTING, for he who doubts is like a wave of the sea driven and tossed by the wind. For let not that man suppose that he will receive anything from the Lord."

There are countless religions, that pray, but not to God. According to the Bible, they pray to false gods. They sacrifice time and energy. They even face specific directions for their prayers to be heard. Their combined prayers and devotion to pray to their gods is enormous, but it remains fruitless. Their act of praying means nothing. Prayer is of no good, except that it be received by a God Who has the power to hear and answer.

Prayer without Faith, profits nothing. NO-THING! Prayer without a God Who hears and answers is fruitless. Thankfully, God, our Father, has the power to do so. He has an ear to hear and His heart is moved and touched by our needs. It is the prayer asked in Faith, that will bring the desired results. Sadly, there are many who do not take the time or the effort, nor do they make the commitment to pray as they should.

A Call to Action

When you're confident that God hears your prayer and that He will answer, it will thrust you into your own secret sacred place that I call prayer. Imagine what would happen in your life, your church and your nation if you would be as committed as those who pray to false gods.

God can't make you pray. I can't make you pray. Your situations might make you pray as a last ditch effort to resolve the issue. However, if you willing seek God and ask for wisdom then you can expect to receive all that God has for you in His Word. The choice is yours.

Spend time right now talking with God about all that is in your heart. He is that friend that will not fall apart when you tell Him everything!

> *"A prayer less Christian is a powerless Christian"*
> *- Billy Graham*

Notes

Whisper Twenty-Nine

John 15:7-8 NKJV says,

"If you abide in me, and my words abide in you, you will ask what you desire, and it shall be done for you. By this my Father is glorified, that you bear much fruit; so you will be My disciples."

As I was getting ready to listen to a message on my ipod, a text came across the screen. It said, *"Connect to Power."* The message I wanted to hear was there, but it couldn't be accessed since there was NO POWER to receive it.

Likewise in the Spirit, God has ALL Knowledge, ALL Wisdom and ALL the Help you'll need. In order to receive the message God has for you there must be a living abiding connection with the SOURCE OF ALL POWER. If you don't have an abiding connection with God, you will not be able to receive from Him. You won't be able to hear from Him.

I am convinced that one of the greatest challenges you will have as a Spirit-filled Christian is learning to accurately distinguish the leading of the precious Holy Spirit. To rightly to discern what is the Lord and what you think you want to hear. It's not easy, but it's definitely worthwhile. This kind of sensitivity is cultivated through praying each day and meditating on the written Word of God. I encourage you to pray in the Spirit and with your own understanding.

Remember the Word of God is the Voice of God. The more acquainted you are with God's Word, the more familiar His Voice will become. You'll be able to recognize in your own spirit what is Him and what is your own desire. Through the written Word of God your mind will become renewed to accept God's way as the right way.

A Call to Action

Cultivate, cultivate, cultivate your connection and dependency upon the Lord. This devotional is intended to direct you to Him. The words I have written point you to Him. He is far greater than anything I could ever say to you directly. Spend time right now putting into practice *John 15:7-8* in your secret sacred place—called Prayer.

When you ask Him to speak to you through His written Word, He will do just that, but you have to ask. It's so that your *"JOY"* will be made full. The greatest JOY comes from knowing that God hears you and answers you. Ask Him!

Notes

Whisper Thirty

Developing your living abiding connection with God requires you to cultivate a sensitivity toward Him in your spirit. These devotionals are called, *"Whispers"* for a reason. God didn't yell them out loud to me. Why, He didn't even write them in the sky and they surely didn't just appear out of nowhere.

These words came from that secret sacred place I call prayer. The precious Holy Spirit literally whispered them to me in my times of abiding in Him and remaining connected to His Word and the Voice of God.

John 15:7 NKJV says,
> *"If you abide in me and my words abide in you, you will ask what you desire, and it shall be done for you."*

Another way for your to develop and maintain spiritual sensitivity is to stay connected to the realm of the spirit throughout your day. Download an App. on your smart-phone or buy the Bible on CD. Listen to the Word of God in your car on your way to work. Listen to the it while you are out and about doing errands.

You're not just limited to listening to the Word of God, go ahead and add worship into the mix of your day. Worshipping the Lord through song or speaking out praises of love to the Lord will also make your spirit sensitive to hear the Voice of God. Abiding in Him is to be plugged into His presence consistently.

I encourage you to make the Lord your priority. As you maintain and keep walking in the Love of God, you can stay connected 24-7. Rest assure knowing that all of Heaven's resources are available to you. The Holy Spirit is constantly with you, ready to talk to you about anything you need and when you need to know it.

A Call to Action

Previously I mentioned that I am asked often how to pray and when to pray. I said to you that it isn't so much about the time frame as it is about just talking with God as you would with your best friend. God is the one to trust with the deepest parts of your heart.

He is the one to help you with what you know needs to be fixed, but it requires you being connected to Him. If you haven't already, spend time right now talking with Him in prayer. Get into the Word of God and let Him whisper into the ear of your spirit what it is that you need to hear.

Notes

Whispers

Section 4

What did You Just Say?

"For assuredly, I say to you, whoever says to this mountain, '
Be removed And be cast into the seas,' and does not doubt in his heart,
But believes those things he says will be done,
He will have whatever he says."
– Mark 11:23

"Far better is it to dare mighty things, to win glorious tri-
umphs, even though checkered By failure...than to rank with
those poor spirits who neither enjoy nor suffer much, Because
they live in a gray twilight that knows not victory nor defeat."
– Theodore Roosevelt

Whisper Thirty-One

According to *Ephesians 6:10:* "*You need to be strong in the Lord and in the power of His might!*" This is not something that comes automatically. It is something that you become as you build yourself up in faith. This happens as you meditate upon the precious Word of God and spend time praying in the Holy Spirit.

Oh Woman of God, you are not to stay wounded. You are to become a mighty warrior! After the death of my husband Gregg, I heard the Lord whisper this to me: *"Keep dreaming and keep reaching."* Life is tough, this is the place where you will experience pain and sorrow, but Christ has overcome for you. No matter where or what you are going through: *"DON'T GIVE UP! Get the plan of God and run with it."*

Place your problems into the Hands of God. When you're under great pressure and conflict in your soul, you must cast the whole of that care upon Him. Roll the burden of that issue upon Him. There is a labouring to enter that rest. If you are still fretting and anxious, then He still doesn't have it from you. He isn't working for you because you haven't given Him anything to work with.

I personally know the point where I have completely rolled that care upon Him: All fear is gone and peace floods my heart. My head may not understand it—but my heart sure does.

I like how John G. Lake said, *"It is not try, but trust."* The man or woman who knows how to stand strong on God's Word in the face of tragedy or all opposition and who works in full cooperation with the Holy Spirit of God is one who will bring the greatest blessings to this earth.

Ephesians 6:10 says,

> *"Finally, my brethren, be strong in the Lord and in the power of His might."*

A Call to Action

The disciples became history-makers. These men turned the world upside down with their faith. They didn't try to be relevant to their culture, instead they did exactly the opposite as they endeavored to become like the original history-maker; Jesus Christ! He was their pattern, not the world they lived in. Trying to resolve any issue in your life by yourself will not produce the results that can be found in Him and in His strength.

Say this with me: *"The Greatest Champion is Jesus Christ. I have His blood line. I have the bloodline of the Master Champion. I let Him express Himself through me. He doesn't know how to be defeated. He doesn't know how to quit. He just knows how to win and I am allowing Him to win through me!"*

Notes _____

_____

_____

_____

_____

_____

_____

_____

Whisper Thirty-Two

God wants to do so much for you! Do you give Him anything to work on? Do you have the care? Do you have the problem? Are you the one trying to figure it all out? All to often, You and me, are the ones limiting what God wants to do in and through us.

1 Peter 5:7 NKJV says,
   "Casting all of our care upon Him, for He cares for you."

Cast your whole care on God. Roll your works on Him. He will take care of it all and He'll even take the weight of it and in exchange for it—He will give you rest. Not only will you enjoy the benefits of rest, but you will have peace until the victory comes. That is what God wants to do for you.

Oh Mighty Woman of God, you will find that if you're willing to trust God and stand against fear or anxiety, that the peace of God will sustain you in the midst of your fiery trials. It maybe difficult at first, because the devil doesn't want you to learn to rest in God's goodness and ability. He doesn't want you to find out that you can really have peace in the midst of the most dire or dreadful circumstances.

Isaiah 26:3 says,
   "You will keep him in perfect peace, whose mind is stayed on you,
   Because he trusts in you."

The only responsibility you have is to keep your mind stayed on Him. The key to victory is for you to roll the care over to Him. *"But Kim, How do I do this?"* When troubling thoughts come your way, cast down those imaginations. Do not entertain the thoughts. For if you do, then those thoughts will lead you. They become the directions you follow.

A Call to Action

This section of Whispers deal with what you have to say. Your confession determines your direction. When any contradicting thought comes, you must say with your own mouth: *"NO!"*

No to those troubling thoughts. Instead speak the Word of God to them. Which Word? Any of the Scriptures listed in this devotional to begin with.

Say this with me: *"God I cast all of this care upon you. I roll the weight of this pressure on you. I believe you will work this to my good. You will make this situation work in my favor."*

It really does work this way. Be willing to stand. You'll find that there is great power extended to you by God. Nothing thrills God's heart more than watching you stand and believe His goodness instead of the lies of the enemy.

Notes
_____
_____
_____
_____
_____
_____

Whisper Thirty-Three

Every morning when you wake up, you should be giving the devil a nervous breakdown! The questions he should be asking nervously is, *"What is she going to do today? Who is she going to impact today? Who is going to be born again because she woke up today?"* Listen really close to this whisper from God for you: *"You were born to RAZE HELL, not raise hell."* Your to completely enforce the destruction of the enemy that Jesus Christ won through His death, burial and resurrection.

This victory wasn't just intended for celebration on Easter Sunday. It is intended for everyday of your life here on this earth. Do what Jesus said you can do. Go give Jesus away and in the process give the devil a headache, all because you just woke up.

2 Timothy 1:7 says,
> *"For God has not given us a spirit of fear, But of power and of love and of a sound mind."*

You don't have to be afraid of the devil. When Lester Sumrall flew into a foreign country he would shout, *"Well devil I am here!"* It has been said that there was a well known minister, who while waking up in his sleep felt the ugly presence of the enemy. He said, *"Oh it's just you."* and then went right back to sleep. That is what no fear looks and sounds like. You need to fear nothing about a defeated enemy.

You are no match for the devil by yourself. But in Jesus Christ you can do anything. Run to the battle of your day, not away from it. Oh Mighty Woman of God, you were made Battle Ready. That is where victories are won and your faith is enlarged. You are His hands. You are His feet. You are His mouth. You are His Arms. Your life is not your own. For you have been bought with a price. The precious blood of Jesus Christ secured your victory.

A Call to Action

1 John 4:17 says,

> "Love has been perfected among us in this: that we may have boldness in the day of judgement;because as He is, so are we in this world."

Jesus' victory over the enemy is yours. I challenge you to go before the Lord in that secret sacred place called prayer and say to Him: *"Lord this is your life and your body. Use me the way you see best. Show me what you want to do through me and I will do it."*

Then begin to spend some time worshipping God. If you're filled with the Spirit, spend time praying in other tongues as the Holy Ghost leads you about your assignment. Don't just do this for today, but let it be known of you to have this operating in you everyday.

Notes
_____

_____

_____

_____

_____

_____

Whisper Thirty-Four

　　　E.W. Kenyon said, *"The Word in lips of doubt and fear is a dead thing; but in the lips of faith, it becomes life-giving, dominant. You see the Word (of God) in the lips of faith becomes just like the Word in Jesus' lips."*

The Word of God, is just that: The very Words of God. Holy men were inspired to write each Book of the Bible. It is the most supernatural Book of God. For it was by the Holy Spirit and His power. There is great influence and anointing upon His Word. That is why it's so important for you to speak them.

John 16:15 says,
　　　"All things that the Father has are mine. Therefore I said that He will take of Mine and declare it to you."

There were many things that the Lord Jesus told the disciples and multitudes of crowds that He had spoken too, but they all didn't understand what He had said. It is amazing to think about how important the words, *"all things that the Father has are mine."* There were thoughts, beliefs, words, desires and then they were to be revealed to you. For your understanding, not for Jesus.

He didn't speak them for Himself, but for you and me. Why? In order for you to pick them up, pray them out, speak them and live by each one of them. The main function of the Holy Spirit in your life is to bring forth the will of God. You are to cooperate with Him in bringing about the plans and will of God in this earth.

God's Words are Spirit. They are eternal and full of Life. These precious Words continue to transcend from one generation to the next. They are powerful, powerful Words. Not just the Words of Christ in the Gospels, but every Word in the Old and New Testament.

A Call to Action

I believe deep within me that it is time for you to say something! Start with letting God know that you know He is greater than any of your circumstances. Speak to your finances and call your checking account FULL. Say, *"I am the head and not the tail. I am above and not beneath."*

Continue to speak out of your heart using your lips to proclaim what it is that you really do believe. Whatever is of a good report, speak those things out. For you will have exactly what you believe you say you will have. *(cf. Mark 11:23)*

If you're not speaking anything different than you have for years, then you will not have anything different in your life. You possess and have what you have spoken and believed from yesterday. *"It is time for you to say something different,"* is what I keep hearing in my spirit for you today.

Notes

Whisper Thirty-Five

Judges 5:21 says,

"The torrent of Kishon swept them away, that ancient torrent, the torrent of Kishon. O my soul, march on in strength!"

Merriam-Webster dictionary defines a torrent as a large amount of water that moves very quickly in one direction. Yet the author of Judges said, *"Oh my soul, march on in strength!"* He didn't think it or hope for it, He said it.

In this life there will be storms. Some storms in the natural are very beneficial. They give water and replenish certain chemicals or vital elements to the soil. However, there are destructive storms and their intent is to destroy everything in its path. Some believe that the storms in your life are sent by God *"To Teach You Something."*

But I say to you Oh Mighty Woman of God, they are sent to destroy you, not to teach you. The storms of life are not sent by God. In *Mark 4:39* Jesus spoke to the storm in the Sea of Galilee and said, *"Peace, be still."* The storm ceased. If God had sent the storm, then Jesus would have been disobeying His Heavenly Father.

The word *peace* here is not the Hebrew word *"shalom."* It's the Greek word *"siopao."* It literally means *"to command someone to be silent"* The silence is involuntary. Meaning you have no say in the matter. You must be quiet, even if you don't want to be silent. Think of how many times the storms in life have shut you up. That has never been God's plan for you. You're supposed to be speaking to the storms.

A Call to Action

It is God Who is at work in within you and He is for you, not against you. Launch out into the realm of the impossible today despite and storms that have silenced you. For God is found in the impossible. Believe for the miraculous because that is what He does.

Tell your soul as the author of Judges did, *"to march on in strength."* I believe there is supernatural grace for you to run your race. Use your faith to speak to storms today. Try things that you've never tried before. Do something you've never done before. Go to a place spiritually that you've never been to before. It all starts here with the words you speak!

Say this out loud with me to your storm: *"Storm, be still. Your out of order! Your voice is now silenced. You must get back in order. Stop your destructive attempt in my life. You have no choice in the matter for I have an assignment from God to complete and there is nothing you can do about it."*

Notes

_____

_____

_____

_____

_____

_____

_____

_____

Whisper Thirty-Six

Oh the prophetic song of the Lord has been in me saying, *"Things are turning around. Around and around, things are turning around and there are things that are returning."* I believe that there is one thing God is trying to get across to you today: He is God. He is the Great *"I AM."* He can work for you and bring the release you need in every area of your life. He is able to do it all by Himself just for you. All you must do is look upon Him.

Acts 3:4-6 says,

> *"And fixing his eyes on him, with John, Peter said, 'Look at us.' So he gave them his attention, expecting to receive something from them. Then Peter said, 'silver and gold I do not have, but what I do have I give you: In the name of Jesus Christ of Nazareth, rise up and walk."*

The crippled man was in need of what money couldn't buy. He needed to be able to rise up. That's what I keep getting in my spirit for The Body of Christ and for you: *"Rise Up."* Within you is the answer. It is what you will be able to say to yourself and others.

Maybe you're in a place that has you crippled or hindered in your life. Circumstances that have you overwhelmed. You go about your day as you always have done, but today there is something different that just has to be done. Like the man sitting at the gate called Beautiful, I say to you, look unto Him. It's not silver or gold that will get you out of the place you're in, but it shall be by your faith in Him. Oh Mighty Woman of God, it's your time to *"Rise Up."* Rise up I say, rise up.

No longer be hindered by the things that you have done or didn't do, but have a fresh new outlook into all the plans that God has for you. As you stand up so tall, you shall be like the gate called beautiful, the place where the crippled man stood up and began to praise God. Praise shall rise up out of you and into all the places you go. There shall be peoples of this earth hear you and see you praising your God, and that is what I see in my spirit for you. A Woman of God rising up in what she has been called to do.

A Call to Action

You can't just sit around anymore. You have a heavenly assignment to do. Before my beloved husband Gregg passed away, he said to not go back to a different type of work, but that I must press on and do what God had called me to do in ministry. I had to and I also had to continue looking upon God to raise me up in every part of my life.

The man at the gate looked upon Peter and John with expectation, as to receive something from them. What he got was more than what he was expecting that day. Encourage yourself today with the words from above: *"Things are turning around. Around and around, things are turning around and there are things that are returning."*

Notes

_____

_____

_____

_____

_____

_____

_____

Whisper Thirty-Seven

Life is tough. This is the only place that you will ever know pain and sorrow, but Christ has overcome for us. No matter where your are or what you've been through: Don't give up! Get the plan of God and RUN with it. It requires strong faith in order to not give up. I heard this down on the inside of me while writing this devotional: *"There cannot be strong faith without absolute and unfaltering trust."*

Proverbs 3:5-6 says,
> *"Trust in the Lord with all your heart, and lean not on your own understanding. In all your ways acknowledge Him, and He shall direct your paths."*

Some words carry heavy meanings. The words alone can be overwhelming. Words like: Tough, Pain, Sorrow or Strong. Yet the key to *"In Life With God"* isn't something you have to work up. It's about your *"Trust"* in God. Smith Wigglesworth said it best, *"I would rather die trusting God, that to live in unbelief."*

I have said it before and will say it again: *"God wants to do so much for you, but you haven't given Him anything to work with."* Trust requires you to give God something. Then once you have given it to Him, leave it right there. That's how you can have absolute and unfaltering trust. You can't expect to go anywhere in victory if you aren't speaking God's Word over your life. I can't do it for you, but you can! As woman I know you know how to speak, now just start speaking the Word.

A Call to Action

You haven't the time anymore to live in defeat. We have a world full of unbelievers in Christ who need to be reached. It's our responsibility to go and tell them that Christ has overcome for them. Sure life is tough. There is pain and sorrow that we must endure. But when the world sees a Mighty Woman of God who hasn't given up despite her circumstances, they will see one with strong faith and absolute, unfaltering trust in her Heavenly Father.

The words that you speak today are the results that you will have tomorrow. Speak about your strong faith and trust in God. Speak about how you lean not to your own understanding. Speak about how God directs your path. Don't be moved by how you feel, only be moved by the Word of God. That is my confession and I am sticking with it, are you?

If I could give only one piece of advice to you it would be this: *"Never, never, never, never give up. It will get better, you get better, as your love and knowledge of Him grows deeper, if you just don't give up and trust Him."*

"When I didn't quit, I won!" - Lester Sumrall

Notes

_____

_____

_____

_____

_____

_____

_____

Whisper Thirty-Eight

When Jesus was raised from the dead, the Father highly exalted Him and gave His Name the power above all names. There is no trouble or sorrow in this world that is greater than the promise of strength in the Name of Jesus. Satan may be the God of this world but he is not GOD! There is no competition or comparison between the two.

Ephesians 1:21 (Aramaic Bible in Plain English) says,
> "Higher than all principalities, rulers, powers, and dominions, and higher than every name that is named, not only in this universe, but also the one that is coming."

I love this translation for it says, "not only in this universe, but also the one that is coming." God has sealed the deal. Everything you could ever have need of He has already met in His Son Jesus. If what you are going through has a name, do not fear it, for His Name trumps it. His Name trumps every disease, ruler, power or nation.

It doesn't matter what your going through, it has to bow to the Name of Jesus. Cancer is a name and it has to bow and give homage to the Name of Jesus. Debt is a name, it must bow. Depression is a name and it must bow. Injustice is a name and it too must bow. *Ephesians 1:19* tells of an exceeding greatness of His power in those who believe. You and I must put faith in that Name as we speak it out or it won't change anything.

A Call to Action

Dr. Ed Dufresne said, *"You've got to speak it to move it."* The responsibility to change anything in your life, comes from you speaking it. Adversity is the enemy's way of telling you that you're too close to a breakthrough. Don't stop speaking until things have changed. It's not solely about you but its all about His Name and faith in His Name that changes everything.

Your confidence in His Name will grant you a boldness that is only reserved for the righteous. It will cause you to speak when you all you want to do is cry. It will cause light to shine in your life where darkness once reigned. It will cause you to stand in a place that you've never stood before.

Say this with me: "*Satan, shut up! I don't serve you. You got served over 2,000 years ago by the one I love and the one I serve, Jesus Christ. He is my Lord and Saviour. The Almighty One. The faithful witness and the firstborn among the dead. He is the ruler of the kings of this earth. He is the One I give my love too. So I speak to cancer, depression, poverty and debt. I speak to injustice, anger and failed government promises and I say in response to them all: Bow in the Name of Jesus. For you must obey that Name.*"

Notes

_____

_____

_____

_____

_____

_____

_____

_____

_____

_____

Whisper Thirty-Nine

In order for you to get a good picture of your life, you must get it from the Giver of Life. God's work in the earth can only be accomplished through His children working with Him. When God has an assignment, He picks a man or woman to do it. It starts out in obedience but when the slightest wind of adversity blows, they often walk away from it leaving God with the plan in His hands and the work uncompleted.

"The boy who is going to make a great man must not make up his mind merely to overcome a thousand obstacles, but to win in spite of a thousand repulses and defeats." - Theodore Roosevelt

One night I was standing in front of the glass window in the Kansas City International Airport looking out into the darkness of the night. Down on the inside of me the precious Holy Spirit reminded me of these Scriptures:

Matthew 5:14-16
"You are the light of the world. A city that is set on a hill cannot be hidden. Nor do they light a lamp and put it under a basket, but on a lampstand, and it gives light to all who are in the house. Let your light so shine before men, that they may see your good works and glorify your Father in Heaven."

You Oh Mighty Woman of God, have been assigned by God to be a light in this world. Spiritual darkness covers this world and you are needed to shine your light in it. Your life must be like a lighthouse that gives definition and clarity. Your light will point those that are lost in the sea of life to Jesus.

A Call to Action

Revelations 3:21 says,

> *"To him who overcomes I will grant to sit with Me on My throne,*
> *as I also overcame and sat down with My Father on His Throne."*

Here is what I hear the Lord whispering to me: *"To him who overcomes fear, selfishness, pride, anger, unforgiveness, lying, greed, lust or anything else you could put in this list, there is victory."* Every woman has temptations or weaknesses that the enemy uses to try to rule over you. They ultimately keep you from fulfilling your assignment.

Know that Jesus too had a flesh that He had to contend with in order to do the Will of God. But it's time for you to get serious about the things that keep you from being fiercely committed to Him. Overcome and do what you know to do. For time is almost over and your reward will be great. Then you shall hear the Lord say to you, *"Well done thou good and faithful servant, enter into the joy of the Lord."*

Notes

Section 5

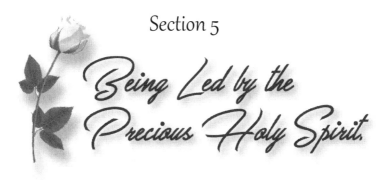

Being Led by the Precious Holy Spirit.

"Now faith is the substance of things hoped for,
The evidence of things not seen."
– Hebrews 11:1

"Faith is our link to the anointing of God."
– Kenneth Copeland

Whisper Forty

Psalms 116:15 says,

"Precious in the sight of the Lord is the death of his saints."

A couple of years ago, a great man of God and I were talking about the death of my husband. He asked me if I was familiar with this Scripture out of Psalms 116:15. I said, *"yes."* He then asked me if I knew what it meant. Immediately I responded that, *"it must be precious to God when His children come home."* He said back to me, *"Well, I'm sure it is precious to the Lord when His children come home, but that is not the meaning of this Scripture."*

This man of God went on to tell me that the Hebrew word for *precious* means: costly, expensive, extravagant. That means *Psalms 116:15* would read as *"precious, costly, expensive in the sight of God is the death of His saints."* He proceeded to tell me that when a believer is worth their salt in the earth, there is then a void when they are gone.

You are a Woman who believes in God. As you grow in the Word of God, your knowledge and understanding of Him grows too. The Holy Spirit is in you and He will give you the desire to reach for more of God. As you begin to let the Spirit of God grow you, He requires you to step out in Faith and release your supply.

A Call to Action

We remember those that have prayed for us. They impacted our lives with their supply. I know a woman that I use to pray with, she actually taught me how to pray. She gave me her supply and now I am giving that supply to you and many others.

Oh Mighty Woman of God, I know that you desire to be a supply in this earth. You desire to leave this world a better place than when you came into it. God can help you accomplish that if you will just ask Him to do it through you.

Ask Him to help you release your supply. He will point you to those that need what you have. Then as you are led by Spirit of God, release it by faith. It will be up to you to obey and release your supply. Say this with me: *"I have a supply. A supply that others need. A supply provided to me by God. A supply greatly increased by my understanding and knowledge of God's written Word. My supply benefits the people God puts across my path each and everyday."*

Notes

Whisper Forty-One

My husband Gregg and I went to San Francisco to minister years ago. While we were there, we went to the Hearst Castle. Are you familiar with this castle? William Randolph Hearst was a newspaper magnate. He built the castle located in the central coast of California. IT was 60,645 square feet. The place is filled with rare and expensive art from all over the world and even ruins from Rome. He had a Roman temple transported to California that was reassembled on site. It was an amazing sight to see.

Every room I went into would cause me to ooh and aah over it. There was just one problem for me. I could only look at things from a distance because everything was roped off do to the value of all his treasures. The chairs were far too valuable to sit upon. The paintings were too costly to touch. Everything was too valuable and untouchable.

2 Corinthians 4:7 says,
  "But we have this treasure in earthen vessels, that the excellence of
  the power may be of God and not of us."

God has placed in you a supply of wealth far greater than that found in The Hearst Castle. What is the treasure that He has placed in you? His presence, His love, Gifts and Talents, the Power of God and the wisdom of the Holy Spirit. All of these things and far more to list has He place in you.

Just like the valuable pieces of the Hearst Castle, we see ourselves as too shy or too busy, so we rope ourselves off from Heaven and our supply from broken and hurting people. Living like that will have you leaving this earth with no supply.

A Call to Action

When you choose to avoid others because you didn't overcome fear in your life it leaves an untapped supply that God needs in this world today. Don't be one who doesn't study the Word of God to increase in knowledge. Don't be one who chooses to not have a working knowledge of God and refuses to bring comfort and cheer the heart of another person. Don't let it be said of you that you were to stingy to give to the church so they could reach out to a lost and dying world with the message of hope and healing found in Jesus Christ.

Every life that Jesus redeemed, He has given His Spirit. The precious Holy Spirit was the source behind Jesus' ministry. He has given you His Word that gives you answers, especially when you are acquainted with the Holy Spirit. He is here to help you bring forth the will of God for your life.

You maybe asking, *"What must I do?"* Simply do what the Lord whispers in your heart. It is how your supply others is released.

Notes

_____

_____

_____

_____

_____

_____

_____

_____

Whisper Forty-Two

When I was growing up I was raised in a house of prayer. My parents were people of prayer. I was raised by them to exalt the Lord and the things of God. As I was growing up my parents always took our family to visit my Grandmother on Saturdays. I recall these visits right up to the Saturday before I got married. She was referred to as a *"shut in"* by the church, one who could not get out to attend church.

Even though my Grandmother had health issues and could not go to church, I never once thought of her being weakly. She had such a strong spirit about her and the presence of God was strong in her life. The one thing I could always count on and expected to see each time was her life in Christ. She has been gone now for over 30 years, but she has left a lasting impression on my heart. I still remember her vividly and still talk about her to this day. She is an example of those who knew that prayer leaves a strong impression upon mankind.

You might not be able to recall all of the Nobel Peace Prize Recipients or great scientists who have contributed greatly to medical breakthroughs or even gifted artists who have created masterpieces, but I say to you that a man or woman who has been made brilliant by the Holy Spirit carries a great supply. For they bring a great lasting impression in this earth.

The supply in them carries the Spirit of God into your local church. The ministers who demonstrate the Power of God and who build your faith, will not be forgotten by you. The things of the Spirit are eternal. If their supply can do that—so can your supply.

A Call to Action

As a Mighty Woman of Faith in God, you carry great importance in this life. Your life matters to all of mankind. You don't have to be in the Five-Fold Ministry or have a great name in ministry to be a supply. Sweet Woman of God, all you need: is to know the Lord and live your Christian life out loud.

Let the Holy Spirit use you to bring lunch to a boss, or to give a card with God's Word on it to a cashier in your local grocery store. One time I went to the post office and the dear lady behind the counter loved a sports T-shirt that I was wearing to represent our local football team. I went home and washed the shirt, put it in a gift bag with a card and gave it to her. She didn't know how to respond.

How is that being a supply? Just giving things away shows love and it blesses people. I have asked countless numbers of people at the drive-thru if there is something I can pray with them about. It is that simple. Make a decision right now to let the Holy Spirit know you want Him to make you a supply of Heaven in this earth.

Notes

Whisper Forty-Three

Never throw in your faith like a towel. Actions like that will cause you to lose the ground you've already gained. Then it's back to the wall. Instead, hold fast to your faith in God. If you've done that recently, just go back to where you left off and continue to believe in Him.

God is willing. He is working on your life. He is working on your behalf. He will not take *"NO"* for an answer and neither should you. How much faith does it take to move a mountain? Just enough to speak to it.

Mark 11:23 says,

"For assuredly, I say to you, whoever, says to this mountain, 'Be removed and be cast into the sea,' and does not doubt in his heart, but believes those things he says will be done, he will have whatever he says."

The victories that I experience in my life, despite any defeats, only come when I speak the Word of God to them and simply believe what I have said. It goes like this: *"Mountain, I tell you to move, be thrown into the sea, get out of my way. You speak to mountains of cancer, diabetes, poverty or depression and tell them to move as they have the wrong address and will not be found in you."*

Maybe you might ask, well do I have to have a certain level or measure of faith in order to speak to a mountain? No you don't. *Mark 11:23* doesn't reference any level or measure. It says, *"but believes those things he says will be done."* Then you possess what you have spoken with no doubt in your heart.

A Call to Action

Hebrews 10:23 says,

"Let us hold fast the confession of our hope without wavering, for He who promised is faithful."

Hold fast your confession of faith and say: I will not feed fear. I will not feed doubt. I will not feed mistrust in my Father who sits on the throne in Heaven. I will not feed those things nor will I add unbelief to my faith. Instead, I feed my beliefs great things. I believe that the greater One lives in me and is working on my behalf. I believe that His Word cannot fail. I believe that the devil is a liar. I believe that God is moving mountains that I have spoken too.

God is bigger than any mountain, so He can move them for you, as you say He can! Actions like these cause you to keep your ground and it proves your hope in God. Take claim to that what is rightfully yours. Then you will experience freedom from poverty, sickness and spiritual death. As a Mighty Woman of God, don't throw in your faith like a towel or wave it as a white flag of surrender to the enemy. Speak to your mountains, for He who has promised is faithful!

Notes

Whisper Forty-Four

What do I do when I've exchanged my faith for sight? Just keep on praying and don't stop. Keep your faith in God and continue to stand your ground in front of the mountain in your life until it has changed. Your enemy willingly works long and patiently to strategize against you. Just be willing to stand longer on the Word of God for your answer and victory. Don't worry about anything just stay in tune with the Holy Spirit.

When things seem impossible and it appears that it would be easier to walk by sight, spend time in worship. Give to Him, your whole heart and all that is within you. One morning I was awakened to a song that reminds me of what to do and it is so beautiful.

There's Something About That Name- Bill Gaither

Jesus, Jesus, Jesus
There's just something about that name
Master, Savior, Jesus
Like the fragrance after the rain
Jesus, Jesus, Jesus
Let all Heaven and Earth proclaim
Kings and Kingdoms will all pass away
But there's something about that name.

A Call to Action

Your simple act of worship will render the enemy strategies ineffective. Jesus, your name is power. Jesus' your name is might. Jesus' your Name will break every stronghold. Oh precious Jesus, your name brings life.

Philippians 2:9 says,

> *"Therefore God also has highly exalted Him and given Him the name above every name, that at the name of Jesus every knee should bow, of those in heaven, and of those in earth, and of those under the earth."*

It is no secret what God can do, He can do anything. All things are possible through Him and those who believe. If your situation looks impossible, He says, *"it is possible but you must believe."* If it has a name, then His Name trumps all other names.

His name trumps cancer, arthritis, depression, oppression, grief, pain, molecular degeneration, sleep disorders, autism, bankruptcy or any other name. If it has a name in this realm then it is subject to change as long as you just believe. You overcome by the blood of the Lamb and the word of your testimony according to *Revelations 12:11.*

Notes

_____

_____

_____

_____

_____

_____

_____

_____

_____

Whisper Forty-Five

In *Mark 4:35-41* we read that it was in fear that the disciples awakened Jesus and said, *"do you not care that we are going to die?"* They spoke to the Master from a place of fear and accused Him of not caring and being neglectful. Surely, you have felt the same way at times?

Of course you have and I use to do it to. But I encourage you to not do that anymore. Instead say what you need to see. Really say what you need to say and that is the Word of God concerning your situation. When you say what you believe instead of what you feel, that is when you will start seeing what God promised you from His written Word and the whispers in your heart.

When I got the phone call from the hospital that my husband Gregg was dying and they didn't think he would make it through to the next morning, I was frightened and my whole body began to shake. I felt so alone. In that moment, I reached into my spirit and spoke out loud what I truly believed. I said to the Lord, *"I have done all that I know to do. I am tired and I am going to lay down to get some rest and trust you."*

The Holy Spirit reminded me of *Mark 4:35-41.* There could not have been a fiercer storm, there could not have been a louder wind blowing and the rains of sorrow were falling on my life. The winds of adversity were blowing hard against my life. I said to the Lord, *"I am going to be like you on the boat in that storm."*

What happened next is amazing. I had a peace flood my spirit, soul and body that wasn't there when I received that call. I didn't really sleep that night because of the tears, but I rested and abandoned my-self to Him. I refused to give into fear. I refused to give into anger. I refused to give into despair.

A Call to Action

John 1:1 says,

> *"In the beginning was the Word, and the Word was with God, and the Word was God."*

Have I been speaking directly to you? Are you waiting for a feeling to let you know that you're going to make it through your storm? Don't look for a feeling, instead, look to the Word of God. Jesus is the Word of God. When you speak His Name things happen. When you remind yourself that His Word says that *"He will never leave you nor forsake you"* but that He is with you always, things happen.

You will have what you say and what you believe. Lift up your hands and say, *"Lord I am going to love you no matter what. I will trust in your goodness for you love me with an everlasting love and I will see your faithfulness from this day forward."*

Notes

_____

_____

_____

_____

_____

_____

Whisper Forty-Six

God cannot promise us that we will not have pain to deal with in this life, but He did promise that He would be there in it and with us and that He would heal. *"Sometimes, that just has to be enough, you know?"* My dad once told me that, *"God is Perfect, Just and Incapable of making a mistake,"* then He went on to say that, *"Our faith in Him is kind of like a three legged stool. If you take away one of these truths, your faith will fall and not be able to stand."*

Our faith in God must rest upon Him being perfect, just and incapable of making a mistake. If you come to God with a heart that sees Him as your last ditch effort then that is a heart which is still untrusting and unbelieving. Choose the promises of God over any pain you have experienced.

Hebrews 11:6 says,

> *"But without faith it is impossible to please Him: for he that cometh to God must believe that He is, and that He is a rewarder of them that diligently seek Him."*

There are those who have said that, *"Time heals all wounds."* Time doesn't heal wounds, God does! Time only separates us from the pain, but God is the healer of your wounds and that Dear Woman of God, requires you to rely upon the promises of God; it is what pleases Him. The precious Holy Spirit whispered to me long ago to *"Build my faith while the sun is shining. Don't wait to build your house of faith in a tsunami, for you might not make it."*

A Call to Action

Dennis Burke said, *"Nobody sees the results of faith without the commitment to live by faith despite what the circumstances look like,"* ask yourself, *"Am I committed to living by faith or am I going to seek shelter in the pain I have experienced?"* Fear will keep you living in pain, but Faith will cause you to see what God sees.

Smith Wigglesworth said, *"If you wait to get faith until you need it, you are too late."* Don't delay building your faith in God. When you do, a grace will come upon you. Grace is God's power and His ability to do what you cannot.

Romans 10:17 says,
   "So then, faith comes by hearing, and hearing by the Word of God."

Discipline yourself to hear the Word of God. That means finding the promises of God in the Bible. Don't just hear them—do them! Apply the promises to your circumstances. Develop your faith by putting pain in its place and moving toward the rewarder of those who diligently seek Him. It's a choice that only you can make for yourself. Choose wisely!

Notes
_____

_____

_____

_____

_____

_____

Whisper Forty-Seven

The greatest thing besides being saved, was becoming a mother. I believe when God created Motherhood, it was the closest thing to His own heart that He could give. As mothers, we watch over and protect our children. We keep them from danger when they are in our presence or when they're not. We place them in His care. We rock our babies to sleep with fevers, cry over them and pray over them. Even when they grow up and become parents themselves, they are still *"Our Baby."*

I thank God for my mother Betty Jane Kroeck. She taught me to pray in the spirit and with my own understanding and she read from the Bible in the mornings before we went to school. Often times I would hear her praying in the Spirit while she would dust and clean the house. I would hear her singing in the Spirit while cleaning the bathroom. She didn't just talk about Jesus, she brought us to Jesus. She brought Him into our everyday life.

All that I am today has been put in there by my precious Momma that Jesus gave to me. She was a supply for me in the spirit. She had a supply to give because she was connected to Jesus: the greatest supply of faith, peace, joy and love the world has ever known.

Near the end of my precious mother's life here on Earth she was placed into a nursing home. Her soul and body were broken down from the effects of Alzheimer, but her spirit was still strong. She was still one with Jesus and her faith was still drawing upon that supply.

A Call to Action

It is very important that you cultivate your faith and love in God. Grow your spiritual relationship with Him. He isn't a lucky charm that you pull out when you need Him. Rather, you know Him and He knows you. If you wait to cultivate that relationship in the storms of life and then try to use your faith it will be too late.

I was with my mother in the nursing home during a visit. I was talking to her about my children and the ministry. I was telling her how bad I felt about being gone so much. She said to me, *"Put them in the Lord's hands. You're working for Him and He is working for you. Give everything to the Lord. Put no trust in any man, only God."* I said to her, *"Do you still feel that way?"* She said, *"Oh Yes. He is as close as you want Him to be, I feel Him more now than I ever have!"*

I have never forgotten those words. When she spoke them to me, she was unable to remember my name, but she never forgot His Name and He never forgot her's. Her faith in God was never shaken. Her supply ran until the very end. It is time for you to operate in your faith supply and be like my Momma: Full of Joy living out *Hebrews 11:1 "Now faith is the substance of things hoped for, the evidence of things not seen."*

Notes

_____

_____

_____

_____

_____

Whisper Forty-Eight

Many years ago the Lord revealed to a man I affectionately called Papa Ron, that Jesus calls His Children (that is you) on Earth, *"Faith Warriors."* That does something on the inside of me. I wouldn't have saw myself like that. Maybe in times that I had won a victory by faith. But as for each and everyday that might be a stretch. It's when you and I get on over into what we think about ourselves, that the thought of being a faith warrior seems nearly impossible.

I Timothy 6:12 says,
> *"Fight the good fight of faith, lay hold on eternal life, to which you were also called and have confessed the good confession in the presence of many witnesses."*

Papa Ron went on to share that a faith warrior is one who overcomes everyday, even through sickness, oppression, difficulties or anything you can name. Your faith in God creates victories. That kind of living is why Jesus sees you as His Faith Warrior. In order to fight the good fight of faith there are three things that Smith Wigglesworth noted about the Apostle Paul: He continued keeping faith no matter the circumstances. He fought the good fight of faith. He finished his course.

A Call to Action

Faith sees things that the natural eye doesn't catch. Seeing yourself as Christ sees you, requires faith. The things you hope for in your life must become a reality long before you see it. Faith allows you to grab hold of it beforehand. Paul was the closest to God in the end because he never gave up on faith. Don't be moved by your circumstances and continue to fight until you have finished the course that God has given you.

You're an overcomer. Learn to be patient with yourself as you are developing strong faith. Dr. Ed Dufresne said, *"People are afraid of needs because we don't like pressure. But if you let the pressure hit your faith, it's all joy knowing that your faith is going to grow and that you will get to the other side."*

Say this with me: *"I am a faith warrior. When the pressures of this life come against me, I let it push up against my faith in God. I am growing and gaining victories. The other side is all I have in my sights. I see things long before my natural eye catches it. I am like the Apostle Paul and will finish my course by not giving up on faith. Circumstances don't move me, only God does. I choose to see myself the way God sees me. I am a faith warrior."*

Notes

Whispers

Section 6

Would You Just Love Me?

"And now abide faith, hope, love, these three:
But the greatest of these is love."
– Hebrews 11:1

"There is no pit so deep, that God's love is not deeper still."
– Corrie Ten Boom

Whispers

Whisper Forty-Nine

The same precious Holy Spirit that inspired the Apostle Paul to write about the divine love of God found in Corinthians is the same Holy Spirit that will inspire you to live your life governed by the truths found in the following verses. If ever there was a time to understand the love of God, it is now. Oh mighty woman of God, I can't emphasize enough, the need for you to pattern your life after the Love of God.

1 Corinthians 13:1-13 AMP says,

> *"If I speak with the tongues of men and of angels, but have not love [for others growing out of God's love for me], then I have become only a noisy gong or a clanging cymbal [just an annoying distraction]. And if I have the gift of prophesy [and speak a new a new message from God to the people], and understand all mysteries, and [possess] all knowledge; and if I have all [sufficient] faith so that I can remove mountains, but do not have love [reaching out to others], I am nothing. If I give all my possessions to feed the poor, and if I surrender my body to be burned, but do not have love, it does me no good at all.*

> *Love endures with patience and serenity, love is kind and thoughtful, and is not jealous or envious; love does not brag and is not proud or arrogant. It is not rude; it is not self-seeking, it is not provoked [nor overly sensitive and easily angered]; it does not take into account a wrong endured. It does not rejoice at injustice, but rejoices with the truth [when right and truth prevail]. Love bears all things [regardless of what comes], believes all things [looking for the best in each one], hopes all things [remaining steadfast during difficult times], endures all things [without weakening]. Love never fails [it never fades nor ends].*

But as for prophecies, they will pass away; as for tongues, they will cease; as for the gift of special knowledge, it will pass away. For we know in part, and we prophesy in part [for our knowledge is fragmentary and incomplete]. But when that which is complete and perfect comes, that which is incomplete and partial will pass away. When I was a child, I talked like a child, I thought like a child, I reasoned like a child; when I became a man, I did away with childish things. For now [in this time of imperfection] we see in a mirror dimly [a blurred reflection, a riddle, an enigma], but then [when the time of perfection comes we will see reality] face to face.

Now I know in part [just fragments], but then I will know fully, just as I have been fully known [by God]. And now there remain: faith [abiding trust in God and His promises], hope [confident expectation of eternal salvation], love [unselfish love for others growing out of God's love for me], these three [the choicest graces]; but the greatest of these is love."

A Call to Action

Get connected with God and His precious Word Whisper to you today. Continue to read the above passages and refer back to them often. Filter your current situation through the hope found above. Be the Mighty Woman of Love that Word of God says you are in Christ.

Notes

_____

_____

_____

_____

_____

Whisper Fifty

1 Corinthians 13 is often referred to as the *"Love Chapter".* Maybe you have read this chapter in several different translations of the Bible. I am sure you've heard great messages taught about this subject. I want to challenge you to perceive it differently, from the thought that *God is Love.* Not like love or love in action, but as another name for Him. He is the One Who introduced the word love to us. He intended for you to understand love as it being Him.

When I read *1 Corinthians 13:1-13* it stirs up three things in me. I am challenged, convicted and confronted to live in a much higher way of interaction with my family and fellow mankind. As you choose this walk, it will become a loftier way and will ultimately demand the death of your selfish ways. Choosing to walk this way will propel you into a deeper walk in Him.

There will be no more looking out for number one [that is you]. You will have to put away taking up a defense for yourself and demanding respect. Instead, it requires great trust in the fact that—God is love. He is by far a better defender of you and can cause respect to come your way as you simply place your trust in Him. Place your trust in LOVE [God], it makes you more like your Father and Jesus, Whose life revealed perfectly this more higher and loftier way of living.

A Call to Action

Listen close to what I am about to say to you: God's design from the beginning has always been that Love would be a name you knew Him by. *1 Corinthians 13:1-13* apart from God is impossible for anyone to accomplish. Your relationship with Him enables you to be more like Him. These Scriptures are His DNA, His nature, it is Who He is.

As a mother, I find great delight in seeing a part of me show up in my children. God is no different when it comes to you. He paid the ultimate price through His Son Jesus Christ. Trusting in God doesn't come by accident.

When you realize that Jesus fulfilled every part of *1 Corinthians 13* before He asked you to, you can't help but to see the possibility of being a Mighty Woman of Love. Flip back one page and continue to read *1 Corinthians 13:1-13* in light of these verses being Who God is toward you.

Francis Frangipane said, *"Trust is not an accident; it is the result of love that pays a price."*

Notes

Whisper Fifty-One

The divine love of God displayed in the life of Jesus Christ demands action in your life. As you live out the destiny He has prepared for you, His life is to become your example. The Bible uses great descriptive words about how Christ revealed a life lived perfectly in Love.

Humble - *Matthew 11:29* says,
> *"Take my yoke upon you, and learn of me; for I am meek and lowly in heart: and you shall find rest unto your souls."*

Servant - *Mark 10:45* says,
> *"For even the Son of man came not to be ministered unto, but to minister, and to give his life a ransom for many."*

Patient - *John 12:27* says,
> *"Now is my soul troubled; and what shall I say? Father, save me from this hour; but for this cause came I unto this hour."*

Merciful - *Matthew 8:2-3* says,
> *"And, behold, there came a leper and worshipped him, saying, Lord if thou canst make me clean. And Jesus put forth his hand, and touched him, saying, I WILL; be thou clean. And immediately his leprosy was cleansed."*

From His birth, death, burial and resurrection from the dead, Jesus fulfilled all of *1 Corinthians 13:1-13*. He laid down his life for you, that you might rise to Him and live. In the same manner, when you are patient with someone and make grace and mercy abound to them or you choose to forgive them and show love, everything changes. No longer will a person who is in your presence have to flinch because they do not feel comfortable around you.

A Call to Action

The love of God in you will make others feel safe around you. Love doesn't demand its own way. Instead, it is patiently bears the burden of others just as Christ did for you. The more you walk in the divine love of God the easier it becomes. Soon you will discover that it is the best way to live life during your time here on Earth.

The more you walk like Christ, the more you become like Christ. As you begin to read Scriptures in light of Who God is in you, the more real He will become. Read *1 Corinthians 13* and in place of the word Love put in God. God is patient. He is kind. He isn't arrogant or rude. He is not easily angered. He bears all things, believes all things, hopes all things and endures all things. God never fails!

As you do this, Oh mighty woman of Love, you can't help but become more in awe of Him. God, in Christ humbled Himself to reach all of mankind with His love. If He did that, then you need too as well. Are you with me on this?

Notes

Whisper Fifty-Two

The love of God is meant to be received and not just acknowledged in your life. Once you have received this love into your life, then it is easily believed. You can't be expected to give away what you do not have. Therefore, if you do not have a revelation of His love or have not encountered His love, then you really can't give love back to Him or to others.

Matthew 22:37-39 says,

> *"Jesus said to him, 'You shall love the Lord your God with all your heart, with all your soul, and with all your mind.' This is the first and great commandment. And the second is like it: 'You shall love your neighbor as yourself.'"*

The faith and love you walk in during your daily life needs to be reaching maturity. It does so as you continue to walk in light of the revelation you have of His love. Look more like the One you are serving each and everyday. Say to yourself, *"I look more like Jesus!"*

Love operating in your life is the touch of God upon you. You will only be like Him because you want to be like Him! You must reach for and go after the Love of God. Ask yourself the question, *"Do I want to fulfill my flesh or my Spirit?"* You will always reap what you are willing to sow.

A Call to Action

Galatians 6:7 says,

> *"Do not be deceived, God is not mocked, for whatever a man sows, that he will also reap. For he who sows to his flesh will of the flesh*

reap corruption, but he who sows to the Spirit will of the Spirit reap everlasting life."

There will always be family and other people that you have to deal with in your life. How you deal with them when no one is looking at you, determines what kind of relationship you will have with them. Begin practicing in your life the outcome you want in their lives and yours. What you do with the hidden things of your heart make all the difference.

Do things in your life by the Grace of God. That includes living in the Divine Love of God found in *I Corinthians 13:1-13.* Do you want Joy in your life? Do you want strength to accomplish what seems impossible? Do you want improved relationships with your family and those who you come in contact with each day? Then you will have to rely on God in order to become more like Him. It only seems difficult accomplish because maybe in certain areas of your life you haven't practiced living by love. Remember what Francis Frangipane said, *"Trust is not an accident; it is the result of love that pays a price."* Pay the price to walk in love today.

Notes

_____

_____

_____

_____

_____

_____

_____

_____

Whisper Fifty-Three

Now wait just a minute Kim, *"You haven't a clue how I have been hurt in my life?"* Oh Mighty Woman of God you are right! I don't have a clue about the hurt in your life, but I do have inside information on how I have been hurt in my life. It is out of that place that I can tell you exactly what happens when your focus is on hurt and not His Love.

Self-pity is the cruelest weapon the enemy has, especially since it's all about you! You are only hurting yourself to stay there because your focus will only be on you. You will find that you only heap continual sorrow upon yourself. Eventually, it will cause you to become sick and angry. The walls of self-pity are filled with bitterness and pain leading only to self-destruction.

A woman who is bitterly painful and full of sorrow will not go to God. In fact, her finger begins to be pointed at Him. She becomes a woman who is no longer a victor, but the ultimate victim. But God! Oh my, how sweet and precious is His love towards us when we feel there is no future. You don't have to live in self-pity, not if you are living your life according to the divine love of God.

A Call to Action

If you're sorrowful and hurt. Maybe angry or bitter, then own up to it. Say it out loud to God, He already knows what you are thinking. Once you say it, then you'll take ownership and I urge you to quickly take it to God.

Oh it will cost you for sure. But God isn't going to make you pay for what you just took ownership of since He already paid the price for you to be released from self-pity in Christ. Instead, He graciously equipped you with His Divine Love to overcome any situation that you might have to deal with in your life.

Start dwelling on the love of God in you. The Word of God is able to divide your thoughts. How quickly you will discover anger, self-pity or any other feelings. How your respond is really up to you. Don't respond based on how you feel, but respond on what you believe from His Word.

I am not the one who said, *"and now abides faith, hope, and love these three; but the greatest of these is love."* I just want you to see what God already sees in you. Go back and read Whisper Forty-Nine and renew your vision for the divine love of God operating in you towards others.

"There is no pit so deep, that God's love is not deeper still."
- Corrie Ten Boom

Notes _____

_____

_____

_____

_____

_____

_____

_____

_____

_____

Whisper Fifty-Four

A life of self-pity is the worst place to be in and it's dangerous. Self-pity is the most destructive weapon the enemy uses. It makes you feel unaccountable to God. After all, you're just feeling sorry for yourself and wishing things had not turned out the way they did. Growing up as a child, my mother worked hard to instill into me to guard my heart against self-pity. She would tell me what Kathryn Kuhlman always said, *"Even God can't help a self-pity woman."*

Why? Because it is a secret thief and self-pity leaves you as a victim of your circumstances. Remaining a victim is a wrong belief to have adapted in your life for it makes you self-centered. Though it seems so innocent it will rob you of your faith and future. As a Mighty Woman of God you are no victim, You are a Victor. Faith works by Love. God's love and your love for others.

If you refuse to allow God to heal you and restore you from the abuse, rejection or whatever caused you to become a self-pitying woman, then it will cause you to recoil. You'll exchange restoration for self-pity and remain weak spiritually and emotionally. It goes on to rob you of your confidence in God and in His love for you. Finally, it will keep you from reaching others with your supply. That is why it is important for you to walk in forgiveness and walk in His love. When self-pity comes you can quickly recognize it and give it no place in your life.

John 10:10 says,

"The thief does not come except to steal, and to kill, and to destroy. I have come that they may have life, and that they may have it more abundantly."

A Call to Action

Why's create a Y in your road. When you live only in the whys, it is a small path on the full road that God is intending for you. State your why. Take ownership of it. But don't stop there. Give it to God. Oh Mighty Woman of God and now of Love, He wants your why's. Change your why's by trusting Him with them.

The love of God causes us to trust Him more. As you trust Him more, you will begin to say things like, *"God I know you, so if I need to know the answer to whys, then I know you will let me know."* Get to the place in your relationship with God that you trust Him with all of your life. It is give and take with Him. When He gives, you take. This enables you to give right back to Him. This is how you live in the love of God.

I've stated before that when I study about the love of God and read *1 Corinthians 13* it does three things in me: It challenged, convicted and confronted me with the realities of Who God is and Who He wants me to be toward others. Become the Mighty Woman of Love that God has created you to be. First for yourself, then for others.

Notes _____

_____

_____

_____

_____

_____

_____

Whisper Fifty~Five

I hear the precious Holy Spirit whispering this statement down in my spirit for you: *"Let Love Rule!"*

Listen carefully to what Paul wrote to Timothy about the last days for we are living in them.

> *2 Timothy 3:1-8*
> *"But know this, that in these last days perilous times will come: for men will be lovers of themselves, lovers of money, boasters, proud, blasphemers, disobedient to parents, unthankful, unholy, unforgiving, slanderers, without self-control, brutal, despisers of good, traitors, headstrong, haughty, lovers of pleasure rather than lovers of God. Having a form of godliness but denying its power. And from such people turn away! For of this sort are those who creep into households and make captives of gullible women loaded down with sins, led away by various lusts, always learning and never able to come to the knowledge of the truth."*

As you read this list, do you see any of these things in you? Corrie Ten Boom said, *"If we behave like the devil in anyway we become allies with him."* How can you even imagine for one minute that you will have authority over the devil if you are acting like him. That is the way of the flesh and not of the Spirit. Be in the truth of Love. Turn from sin. Don't give any excuses if you are behaving in a boastful way. Rather seek forgiveness, that the love of God may abound more richly in you.

If you love yourself more than others and even God, seek forgiveness and change. If you are unloving, unholy, revile and are disobedient to parents or those in authority seek forgiveness and change. Now do you see why the precious Holy Spirit of God is saying, *"Let Love Rule?"*

A Call to Action

Do not be known as a Woman who refuses to say she is sorry or unwilling to forgive. If you have any of the items listed above operating in your life it's no wonder why God is unable to move in your midst. Instead of being like that why not *"Rule from a place of Love."*

Let love be the beginning and the end of every decision you make. Make it your immediate response in every matter. Love confronts, love disciplines, love shows mercy, love gives and it protects. Let everything you do, be from the place of Love and it will bless your life. Forgiving a person when they do you wrong does not make that person right. It just makes you free and Freedom is the place where God wants you to be.

Notes

Whisper Fifty-Six

When my husband Gregg and I went to Florida to minister. The Pastor put us in a really nice hotel right on the beach. On a very dark night, I was sitting out on the deck. The fresh salty breeze was coming off the ocean and I could hear the waves crashing against the rocks and washing over the shore. As I listened to the ebb and flow of the waves I heard the precious Holy Spirit whisper this into my heart: *"The love of God is like the ebb and flow of the ocean waves. It splashes on the shore and rolls back into the ocean. His love rolls over the shore of your heart and you can't help but to respond by sending love back His way. He loves you and you love Him. Respond to His most wonderful love."*

1 John 4:19 says,
    "We love Him because He first loved us."

Oh Mighty Woman of Love, He first loved you! It's impossible to love Him without first experiencing His love. That is the only way for you to even love back. I have challenged you to become more like *1 Corinthians 13:1-13* on purpose for two reasons: First that you might receive the love of God shed abroad in your heart. Secondly, that you might share that same kind of love with others.

A Call to Action

The words to the song, *"Here is Love"* by Evan Roberts say: "*Here is love, vast as the ocean, loving kindness as the flood, when the prince of life my ransom shed for me His precious blood, who His love will not remember, who can cease to sing His praise? He shall never be for-*

gotten throughout Heaven's eternal days. On the mount of crucifixion fountains opened deep and wide. Through the floodgates of God's mercy flowed the vast and gracious tide, grace and love like mighty rivers poured incessant from above. Heaven's peace and perfect justice kissed a guilty world in love."

Do you want to love God more? Then allow the ebb and flow of His love roll over the shore of your heart. Allow the precious love of God to come into every area of your life. First you receive that God kind of Love in your heart and then you allow it to go out to others. That is how you stay in the love of God towards your family and all of mankind.

Notes

Whisper Fifty-Seven

You receive love in order to love. Spend time worshipping God. Thank Him that He first loved you and that you are able to love Him back. I want you to know that God is consistent and faithful. You can always depend upon God's love. Both for you and in how you can love others.

Love is one of the nine fruits of the Spirit. Their also characteristics of who Christ is in you. The more you love God the more you will act like Him. The more you allow the love of God to govern your decisions and actions, the more you will look like Christ. By receiving this love into your life, you end up developing great characteristics that can be pulled up at anytime.

Galatians 5:22-23 says,
> "But the fruit of the Spirit is love, joy, peace, longsuffering, gentleness, goodness, faith, meekness, temperance; against such there is no law."

Once you are in Christ, the precious Holy Spirit sheds His divine love in your heart. Enabling you to love Christ, but also others. Love is a fruit of the Spirit. It is a signature fruit. Now you have the ability to love just like Jesus loved, no kidding, just like Jesus.

Sure you have struggled to love and thought there has to be an easier way that isn't such a struggle. You need to know that your flesh will always be actively opposed with God. The way love works is for you to just yield to it. Just like any other fruit of the Spirit, you have to make a withdraw from it. You release it and give it away. Even if another person doesn't ask for it. It won't feel natural at first, but as you yield to love it will become easier and easier.

A Call to Action

There is no excuse for you not to walk in Love. Give away love and God will give more of His power to you. By walking in the Divine Love of God, you'll become a force field of protection. Similar to a cushion or insulation against all evil.

According to *1 Corinthians 13*, Love believes the best of everyone. In dealing with people, you will need to understand that this is not Heaven. People don't walk around with halos over their heads. Instead, people can be cruel, untrusting, crusty and down right hateful.

A key to walking in Love that the Lord revealed to me is: Love believes the best of every person. If you'll believe the best about people, you'll get the best from them. That kind of supernatural love is in you. But you must release it and let it go in order to touch the world for Jesus.

Let today be the day that you rekindle a new love for God and Jesus and the precious Holy Spirit. By keeping it real, it will be real in you.

Notes

_____

_____

_____

_____

_____

_____

_____

_____

Whisper Fifty-Eight

How many times have you opened up your refrigerator and took out a piece of fruit that you wanted? Silly, I know, but it proves my point. As a Mighty Woman of God and Love, your spirit has been regenerated. *2 Corinthians 5:17* points out that if you are in Christ you're a brand new creation. Before you understood that He first loved you, it was impossible for you to love others the way God intended you to love them. As vital as the blood flow is to the heart, so is the Love Flow to your new spiritual heart.

In the same manner that you reached into your refrigerator to get a piece of fruit, it is time for you to reach into the new creation that you are and pull up what is needed to respond in love towards all of mankind. The more you reach for the character of Christ found in the nine fruits of the Spirit, the more you will mature in them.

Everything you have need of, is found in God. Desire to live out of your spirit and not your flesh. Let your spirit man rise up on the inside of you and hear what the precious Holy Spirit of God whispers into your heart regarding the situation you are facing today. Spirit leads spirit. Allow your spirit to be led by Him. Yield to what He is showing you to do. The rewards you receive both in this life and the one to come, will be a direct reflection of your desire to mature in them. Maturity comes in what you are reaching for.

A Call to Action

2 Peter 1:2-3 says,

> *"Grace and peace be multiplied to you in the knowledge of God and of Jesus our Lord, as His divine power has given to us all*

things that pertain to life and godliness, through the knowledge of Him who called us by glory and virtue."

Be a good receiver and accept the love of God. If you mess up, be quick to repent. Don't focus on your mistake, but quickly receive the Love God has for you at all times. Read *1 John 1:9-10*. When you do those three things it will strengthen the humility that is defined in your character by the love of God.

Bear great fruit in your life and especially the greatest one of all, Love. It is not just all about you, but it is Christ in you. Yield to Love. Pull on it when you want to just yell at someone. When the love of God is developed in your heart to the point that it's your first response, that is when the nature of God is changing you. Get yourself to the place where you know that you're a child of God, that you know He loves you and that you receive His love for you.

Notes

Whisper Fifty-Nine

No one loves you like Jesus. He watches over your life with great care and protection. He has invested in you. If you work with Him, He will see to it that you will bring Him a great return. You can't out give God. He will reward you for how you have accepted love and expressed love. I've always loved people. Looking back I can see that it is a special grace upon my life.

However, there was a time when it seemed like family, friends and people in general were very insensitive and unkind. Furthermore, it seemed they were clueless and uncaring about the way they were treating me. I began to become very hurt and eventually hardened my heart. It led me to become very untrusting toward people.

Love began to wane in me and then I noticed that things never seemed to change. As I began to pray about this, I asked the Lord to show me what happened. He revealed to me how it all began and what it did to me. I asked how I could change it and He whispered the answer to me.

This is what I live for: to hear the whisper of the precious Holy Spirit revealing truth and knowledge to me. He gave me 1 Corinthians 13:1-13. He went on to whisper that love believes the best. That was my answer and with this instruction the only way to love again is to trust again. As you believe the best, you'll get the best of people and your heart will love again. I am so thankful for the Holy Spirit, the Spirit of Wisdom who knows everything.

A Call to Action

Galatians 5:6 says,
> "For in Christ Jesus neither circumcision nor uncircumcision avails anything, but faith working through love."

Hebrews 11:6 says,

> *"But without faith it is impossible to please Him, for he who comes to God must believe that He is, and that He is a rewarder of those who diligently seek Him."*

Your life will only function in its fullest capacity, when you abide in the place of love. That's where the power of God is found. It's where your faith in Him will abound. You must love better. I want you to know that you can increase in love because Christ dwells in you. His desires is for divine love to be maturing in you.

I hear the Spirit of God whispering this for you: *"You have to be convinced that God is for you and that He loves you. He wants you to know that His love must go very, very deep. It has got to be a revelation in you. It is very different than when someone says your mother loves you; and you say of course, she is my mom yet I say to that is how most people look at my love for them."* Believe that God loves and that He is not mad at you. Faith in God works by Love.

Notes

_____

_____

_____

_____

_____

_____

_____

_____

_____

Whisper Sixty

You live in a world of hurting people. Someone once said, *"Hurting people, hurt people."* Even Jesus said it was impossible for you live on this earth and offenses not to come your way. It is important for you to maintain a healthy heart spiritually.

Free yourself from offenses and unforgiveness in order to maintain a healthy love of God operating in and through you. Your spiritual life must be in contact with God. He is able to heal you from offenses and show you the way out. The Lord whispered to me years ago, *"Do you want to be like the one who hurt you or do you want to be like the one who died to heal you?"* I want to be like Jesus! What about you?

Luke 17:1 says,
> *"Then He said to the disciples, "It is impossible that no offenses should come, but woe to him through whom they do come!"*

Holding onto offense that were created by others, only makes you become more like them. The only way to be whole and loving is to stay connected to the one who is whole, perfect and who is love! Oh Mighty Woman of God and Love, as a believer if you have knowingly offend someone, for the sake and cause of Christ, go make it right with them. The end of *Luke 17:1* warns you if you choose not too.

A Call to Action

The Lord is your reliable source for peace in any circumstance of life. You're charged by God to guard your conduct from causing others to be offended. Immaturity in this area will keep you from experiencing the fullness of God's power in your life. Walk in such a way that peace and love toward mankind is dependent upon your response to *1 Corinthians 13:1-13*.

I end this devotional with a prayer that Paul wrote to the Church at Ephesus. I trust that these words have Challenged You, Convicted You and Confronted you with the truths that only God can whisper into your heart.

Ephesians 3:14-21 says,

> *"For this reason I bow my knees to the Father of our Lord Jesus Christ, from whom the whole family in heaven and earth is named, that He would grant you according to the riches of His Glory to be strengthened with might through His Spirit in the inner man. That Christ may dwell in your hearts through faith; that you, being rooted and grounded in love may be able to comprehend with all the saints what is the width and length and depth and height. To know the love of Christ which passes knowledge, that you may be filled with all the fullness of God. Now unto Him who is able to do exceedingly abundantly above all that we ask or think, according to the power that works in us. To Him be glory in the church by Christ Jesus to all generations, forever and ever."*

Notes

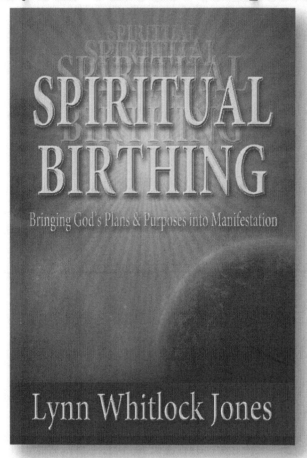

Made in the USA
Columbia, SC
09 December 2017